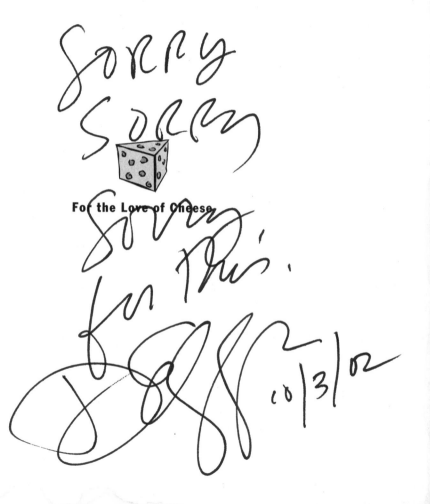

For the Love of Cheese

SORRY SORRY Sorry for This.

10/3/02

For the Love of Cheese

The Editors of *Might* Magazine

BOULEVARD BOOKS, NEW YORK

For the Love of Cheese

A Boulevard Book / published by arrangement with
Might Magazine

Printing History
Boulevard edition / August 1996

The Putnam Berkley World Wide Web site address is
http://www.berkley.com

ISBN: 1-57297-153-3

BOULEVARD
Boulevard Books are published by The Berkley Publishing Group,
200 Madison Avenue, New York, New York 10016.
BOULEVARD and its logo are trademarks
belonging to Berkley Publishing Corporation.

Printed in the United States of America

10 9 8 7 6 5 4 3 2

For the Love of Cheese

a cheese primer

Cheese is not only good fast food, but, goddammit, it's the very cement that holds this nation together. You see, cheese is everything big and flashy and shiny and squishy. Cheese is gaudy and silly and cheap. Cheese is soft-edged, flamboyant, dopey, overdone, loud. Cheese is something that, until recently, when the British started going simply apeshit with the idea, this country had produced better than anyone else. Everywhere else you had these antiquated notions of class and style and decorum, where people would be remiss to, say, wear a pair of biking shorts to lunch at IHOP. But not here. Here, we have always been a nation happy—absolutely thrilled!—to be considered corny. Hell, we've been grinning ear to ear about it for over 600 years (or whatever). We've been renowned for being tacky, geeky, awkward, lacking grace or taste or restraint. We liked our stuff sparkly and obvious. Cheese. Yes, we liked our cheese.

Of course, cheese has never been relegated to one particular segment of the population. No, it's not just those you choose to call "big-hair-mall-rat-semi-suburban morons," not just those who drive Camaros and drink RC Cola products. It's much more. It's us. It's part of our daily lives, part of ourselves—each and every one of us. Yet we often hide our cheese. We put it in the closet and turn out the light and then go rent movies starring Kevin Bacon. But why? Cheese has been too long hidden away. We've decided to "out" cheese, let it breathe, which is, of course, something you're supposed to let cheese do. We are here to celebrate cheese as that happy medium between being fun and being an imbecile, the razor-sharp line between being charmingly goofy and being someone you want to beat with a mallet. We are going to stand up and say, "These are the cheesy things we know. Here they are!

A TAXONOMY OF CHEESE

getting it straight

So now let's get started. Surely we all know of the concept of "cheese." And we know of the popularity of its attendant modifier, "cheesy," employed in statements like, "That is *so* cheesy." We also know that some things are quote unquote cheesy while others are not. But how we define what is cheesy varies from country to country, state to state, person to person, and thus is cause for much confusion, debate, and at least three regrettable accidents in western Pennsylvania. What we need, then, is a Linnaean taxonomy of cheese, a way to celebrate and classify the enormous diversity of cheese in the known universe. After all, things are cheesy in lots of different ways. For example, the Velveeta Cheese Family includes fuzzy dice and pink waitress uniforms and cat's-eye glasses and early Bette Midler. The Dork Cheese Family contains the Travelling Wilburys and the Hogan Family and Bill Gates and post-1985 Bette Midler. The Evil Cheese Family includes things like styrofoam, marine park dolphin shows, ghetto marketing and Al D'Amato. Frederick's of Hollywood red satin teddies are a particular species of ersatz fromage akin to that wobbly slab of pale yellow stuff you get on Subway sandwiches. In this section we will dissect those more common and base forms of cheese so that we may then move on to a higher level of cheese, the Supracheese, representing a genus of cheesiness that does not stratify or divide, but instead says "Come one and all, it's all right. Follow me

velveeta cheese

This is the typically cheesy stuff, the tack-tack-tacky cheese, too obvious to care much about. This is the cheese of the great unwashed, the cheese you might find on QVC or discussed by the likes of Jay Leno. It is common and base, and almost uniformly disagreeable. In sharp contrast to Supracheese, upon which we base most of this tome, Velveeta cheese is not usually enticing, but rather cheap and unappealing. Gaze upon this cheese and despair.

Animal sidekick movies

Long-handled combs

Car ornamentation

Tank tops

Tube tops

Crop tops

Hot tubs

Limos

Local TV news

Polka

Penthouses

Cruises

Cruising

Myrtle Beach

Lambada!

Ribbed condoms ("For her pleasure")

Satin

Palm trees

Fuzzy dice

Pink waitress uniforms

Cat's-eye glasses

Early Bette Midler

Planet Hollywood

Wearing fraternity stuff after college years

Wedding reception bands

Soccer haircuts

Bugle Boy commercials

The Bud girls—e.g., beer posters with large-breasted women

P.D.A.

Dog or cat pictures/calendars/coffee mugs/bumper stickers/mouse pads

Wrist corsages

Men in full-length fur coats

Red power suits

New Jersey

Ski bunnies

Asking a woman if she's ever been a model (Bonus: she's 5' l")

Telling a man you used to be a model (Bonus: you did it during school breaks!)

Leather pants

Dabbling in pornography

Extortion

Flexing your muscles (Bonus: in front of a mirror)

Scouting for babes (Bonus: referring to their locations as "one o'clock")

Paying for sex

Cleaning guns for fun

Making out with a game show host

White shoes

Lighting your farts

Christmas music the day after Thanksgiving

Listening to the album on the way to the concert

Listening to the album on the way back from the concert

Giving a friend a picture frame with a cute picture of you both in it

Leather

Lace

Leather & Lace

Toga parties

Decorating with a Southwest motif

Talking about John Travolta's comeback and pretending that you knew it all along

Nude pantyhose

Tanning lotion

Tanning booths

Jagermeister on tap

The phrase "24/7"

Reunion tours

Leg warmers

Neon illumination under your car

Beauty contests (Bonus: beauty contests held in malls)

Malls

Strip malls

Strip malls across from other strip malls

The Jersey Shore

Stating that you can't find condoms large enough to accommodate your manhood

Flip-flops

Ponytails behind bald heads (Bonus: ponytails in the back, short and fluffy on top)

"Hard Copy"

"Cats" or "Les Misèrables" sweatshirts

Pictures in photo stores

Pictures in photo albums when you buy them

Gloves with the fingers cut off, Michael Jackson style

Gloves with the fingers cut off, Madonna style

Prince style

Couples wearing matching designer sweat suits

Rodent-sized dogs

Videotaping key sites on a vacation

Videotaping your wedding

Dancing on the bar

Wet and Wild cosmetics

News anchorpeople chitchat

Weathermen

Yanni

Bank commercial theme songs

Child actors

Acid washed anything

"Members Only" anything

Airline magazines

Used car commercials that feature the owner's mother (Bonus: she's dressed in a funny/festive costume)

Eye shadow

IHOP

"Co-ed naked sports" T-shirts

The young adult romance section in libraries

A stuffed animal collection displayed in the back window of your car

Ed McMahon

Applying makeup in public

Tie-dyes

Using "rock" as a verb (Bonus: in the past tense)

Giving yourself a cute nickname, because no one else will ("Hi! You must be Kate." "Yeah, but you can call me KiKi.")

Limbo

Hello Kitty

dork cheese

Dork cheese is a step up from Velveeta cheese, but that step is a wee little baby step. What differentiates Dork cheese is that the poor saps who make use of it usually don't know any better. Everyone knows a dork or two, right? Well, Dork cheese is their stock in trade; it's what makes them what they are. Whereas Velveeta cheese might make a normal person angry, Dork cheese evokes feelings of pity. Like the weather, death or the likelihood that Tabitha Soren will say stupid things, we cannot help Dork cheese. It is there and we are sorry for it, but we can't do a thing about it.

Books on tape

Anything "from Hell" (e.g., "The Date from Hell")

Anything "on acid" (e.g., "It was like the Wizard of Oz, on acid")

Casual Day

Ferns

Fern bars

Aerobics

Faking being drunk

Salvador Dali posters

"Been there, done that"

"… NOT!"

Cats on leashes

Fanny packs

Small Bic lighters

Michael Jordan merchandise

Name tags

Screen savers

Jean jackets

Pictionary

Going to the bathroom with someone else

Non-dairy foods

Photos of famous monuments

Striped socks

Zima

Dissing Zima

Theme parties

Doing shots

Coupons

Sweater sets

Bookmarks

Public display case exhibits with things like WWI propaganda buttons

Watches that are status symbols

Watches that are fashion statements

Calculator watches

Watches with depth detectors and compasses

Actually putting bread in a breadbox

Couple dancing

Party invitations

Wash and fold

Groupies (Bonus: being one, dissing them)

Getting really into the music of a new boy/girlfriend

Matching socks to your tie

Mouthing to people "Shut Up!" when you're on an important phone call

Researching your family's lineage

Having a stranger take a picture of you and your sweetie

Being surprised when that picture doesn't turn out well

Magnets

Havin' clothes just for around the house

Celebrating pet birthdays (Bonus: presents and party favors … for the pet!)

Tying rubber bands around your pant cuff before biking

Practicing your signature

Reading the directions

Arts & Crafts

Shower organizers

Washcloths that are gloves

Hanging your high school graduation tassel from your rearview mirror

Describing the way you are, e.g., "I'm the kind of person who …"

Visiting your old college or high school and marveling how much everything has/has not changed

Wearing a sticker after giving blood

Mayo on the side

Wearing work boots with shorts

Dressing up as the opposite sex on Halloween

Sending Christmas cards (Bonus: with pictures of the dog!)

Putting your socks on first

Using the metric system

Sock drawers

Happy Birthday signs printed on dot matrix printers

Saying, "You're funny," after laughing at someone's joke

Flirting by e-mail

Refusing to go out unless you're on the guest list

Keeping your albums and CDs in alphabetical order

Changing your regional accent in accordance with a move to a new part of the country

Greatest hits records and "best of" book anthologies

Calling the surface of your nail a "nail bed"

Painting pictures on your nail beds

Jeeps with Christmas wreaths in the tire spot

Wearing the requisite color on holidays (Bonus: making it red on Valentine's Day!)

Potpourri in the bathroom

Forming a train on the dance floor

Jeans with revealing holes

Making holes in your jeans

Turtlenecks

Dickies

Pleated Chinos

Slacks

Cosby sweaters

Naming bars on college campuses "The Library"

Background songs on answering machines fading out, then back in when you're finished talking

"Top Ten Reasons …" T-shirts

Still saying "Are we having fun yet?"

Holding a beer mug with your thumb over the handle and your pinkie below (Bonus: holding a can like that)

Wearing galoshes over shoes

Child prodigies

Loafers

Knowing what size tire your car takes

Not "being yourself" before your morning coffee

Not "being yourself" before your morning Diet Coke

evil cheese

Evil cheese is like other cheese in its ability to provoke a cringe or a shudder, but Evil cheese is otherwise much more powerful and pernicious. Sure, we can share a chuckle about things like kids on leashes and direct mail, but we also must recognize that the by-products of such cheese can cause harm—that, like laughing along with funnyman Rush Limbaugh, Evil cheese is at first enticing, but leaves a bitter aftertaste.

Black fast food commercials

Car commercials that pretend that their assembly line workers love their jobs

Commercials that list the product's web site at the end

Watching golf on TV

Calling all movies "films"

Rock criticism that uses the word "seminal"

Being a vegetarian who only eats "chicken and fish"

Using dead presidents to sell used cars

Being psyched you have a friend of a different race

Sleeping with someone else the night before your wedding

Answering the phone and pretending it's not you

Not letting people merge in front of you

Reluctantly letting them merge, and then riding their ass

Breaking something at a friend's house and not telling them

Breaking something at a friend's house and fixing it just enough so that the next time someone touches it and it falls apart, it'll look like they broke it

Gun expos

Secretarial school

Screaming "You suck" at the opening band

Getting your friends drunk when they don't want to

Visiting your parents and having to ask for the car

Gynecologists

Old, male gynecologists

Health clubs with windows that face the street

People on Stairmasters in health club windows

Throwing up at a bar

Throwing up and ordering another drink

Walking real slow in the crosswalk

Walking real slow in the crosswalk and glaring at the people in the cars because they're bad polluter types and you're a free spirit, at one with the earth

Walking real slow in the crosswalk on your way to your own car

Al D'Amato

The Pentagon

Kissinger

Pronouncing French expressions like 'double entendre' the correct French way, so no one knows what you're saying

Jargon

Getting the disease you thought you'd probably get

11

Bands that sound exactly like other bands

Complaining about your job, but never doing anything about it

Staplers without staples

Ghetto marketing

Being real nice to people—bus drivers, janitors, cops—who you assume hate their jobs and aren't as happy and fulfilled and smart as yourself

Gym teachers who insist on personally handing towels to kids getting out of the shower

Parents yelling "Take him down!" from the sidelines of grade school soccer games

Girls with no zits bonding over zit problems on skin cleanser commercials

Movies created for soundtracks

Dissing the Midwest

Tickling someone immediately after they say they aren't ticklish

Mean doctors

Thinking you're one of the elite

Throwing stuff off freeway overpasses

Dressing siblings identically

Stage moms

Hallmark holidays like "Sweetest Day"

Quizzes in women's magazines

Strangers who tell you to smile

Answering the phone with the company slogan

Answering the phone "Bass Tickets, we prefer Visa"

Entertainers who dabble in politics

Politicians who dabble in entertainment

Public service announcements that show little kids playing and being cute and then mention that they were killed by a drunk driver or by an awful sickness for which there is no cure

Christian magazines

Car commercials emphasizing trust, security and family

Saying "This is America"

Adding "...the land of the free!"

MacNamara

Public urination

Having one non-white person in TV show's ensemble cast, because, like, sure there are minority doctors and stuff, but not *too* many, you know?

Helicopter spotlights in L.A.

Personal assistants

Homeless jokes

Human-shaped targets at firing ranges

Calling secretaries by their last name ("Ms. Jones, can I see you?")

White hip-hop enthusiasts saying "Whassup nigga?"

Finding redeeming qualities in Hitler

Finding redeeming qualities in Strom Thurmond

Fake concern

Movies about gangs and drug dealing that are purportedly about how bad it all is, but that somehow still manage to make the whole thing sort of glamorous—oops!

Pollsters

Buying things, like 1970s clothes, that you don't like, in order to fit in

Veal

Taking pictures of "cute" natives while vacationing in the Third World (Bonus: showing the pictures to your rich, white friends over chardonnay and brie)

Doctoring photos in women's magazines

Tract housing

Chanting

Kissinger

This page left blank by request of the
United States Marine Corps.

SUPRACHEESE!

But those kinds of cheese listed above aren't the kinds of cheese we'll be concerning ourselves with today. Our kind of cheese is finer, more subtle, better aged—delicious! Our brand of cheese is cheesy, sure, but it's also fun. Fun, fun, fun! It's cheese we all share, cheese for which we all have an undeniable soft spot, the kind of cheese of which we are not afraid. It's the kind of cheese you wish you could take a nice long bath in, while wearing a hat. Let's begin here, and follow the master Supracheese list throughout—it'll be in reverse type, on the right-hand side, right near your grocer's freezer.

1. Baton twirling

2. Going to the bathroom while you're on the phone

3. Asking for a doggie bag in a restaurant

4. Having the food wrapped in foil shaped like an animal (Bonus: it's a swan!)

5. Commercials that rap

6. Kids' commercials that rap

7. Oversized greeting cards

8. The sets for local TV news

9. Cafe art

10. Personalized stationery

11. Personalized key rings

12. Personalized key rings with a funny name that is not yours (Bonus: the funny name is something silly, like "Ricardo" or "Madge!")

13. Growing out your hair

14. Toothpastes with the pump

15. Sneakers with the pump

16. Talking with a toothpick in your mouth

17. Putting a cigarette behind your ear

18. Sticking a pen under your nose to make a mustache

19. Moon boots

20. Wet suits

21. Wet suits that are shorts

22. Mount Rushmore

23. Ads that spoof Mt. Rushmore by putting sunglasses on their faces

24. Grab bags

25. The "grab bag" section of the newspaper

26. Forgetting someone's name and saying, "I'm really bad with names"

27. Actually remembering someone's name but pretending to forget because they don't look like they remember you

28. Telling someone they look like a famous person

29. Starting any story with "a college buddy of mine once …"

30. Stealing ashtrays from restaurants

31. Stealing toilet paper from restaurants

32. Airport gifts

33. Prewrapped airport gifts

34. Stealing somebody's joke and not giving them any credit (Bonus: he/she is standing next to you)

35. Commenting on someone's height

36. The word "groin"

37. Kneeing someone in the groin

38. Having a hernia

39. Quoting "Sixteen Candles" ("No more yankee my wankee—the Donger need food.")

40. Something "to boot" ("You get all that … and a free meal to boot!")

41. Floral arrangements

42. Floral arrangements that come in mugs you can save

43. Bunk beds

44. Pillow shams

45. Party hats

46. Impersonating Groucho Marx (with invisible cigar)

47. Pretending you're Italian

48. Retelling a stand-up comic's routine and pretending it happened to you

49. Sanding wood

50. Pouting

51. Running and then sliding on ice

52. Nooners

53. Lapels

54. Crotchless anything

55. Quickies

56. Busting on Hagar

57. Defending Hagar

58. Tongue tricks

59. Do-si-do's

60. Playing with dolls

61. Running with the bulls

62. Running with the cows

63. Eating toast when you're sick

64. Kicking sand in wimpy guys' faces

65. Mashing potatoes

66. Planning ahead for the future

67. Voting for yourself in the general election

68. Dancing with a mop

69. Taking advantage of a drunk mop

70. T-Bills

71. T-Birds

72. T-Squares

73. Gambling (Bonus: teaming up with a Lady Luck)

74. Dating single moms

75. Riding turtles

76. Scaring small children

77. Scaring pediatricians

78. Scaring podiatrists

79. Putting your arm, instead of a cone, in the cotton candy machine

80. Calling in sick for no reason (Bonus: then showing up for work)

81. Sleeping in

82. Holding your pee so you can go in the shower

83. Keeping up on current events

84. Wearing only a tie to bed

85. Making good use of that tie

86. Car dancing

87. Flashing your brights as opposed to honking

88. Weaving

89. Waving to people (Bonus: you have no clue who they are)

90. Asking only rhetorical questions

91. Thinking about sex at work

92. Using kitschy language for effect (e.g., brewski, hoser, OPP, Pac Man Fever)

93. Playing darts (Bonus: when your friend turns around you put all the darts right in the bull's-eye and then act like you threw them!)

94. Chalking your cue stick after every pool shot

95. Dating models

96. Doorknob fun in general

97. Charades

98. Respecting the President

99. Marching (Bonus: goose step)

100. Gargling

101. Earth Day

102. Talking in a foreign dialect (Bonus: acting like it's normal)

103. Putting your leg in a cast at the ski slope to get sympathy from the babes

104. Tying your enemy's shoelaces together

105. Rolling your eyes

106. Burning someone's hair in class

107. Remaining seated during the now obligatory standing ovation at the symphony/theater/concert

108. Joining fan clubs (Bonus: Gallagher's, John Tesh's, Abe Vigoda's)

109. Pirouettes

110. Gargoyles

111. Playing in quicksand

112. Chewing on metallic gum wrappers

113. Bumper cars (Bonus: hitting someone you think is cute!)

114. Cruises

115. Spelunking (Bonus: without map and compass)

116. Snorkeling

117. Using scuba equipment, for any reason, in Iowa

118. Conditioning your hair before the shampoo

119. Limbo (Bonus: practicing limbo in your spare time)

120. Fun with dynamite

121. Honking your horn to the music on the radio

122. Watering those dry spots on the lawn

123. Shellacking

124. Pissing off the mob

125. Turning up the television really loud and when somebody screams "Turn it down!" you respond "What? I can't hear you!"

126. Dabbling in art

127. Quoting lines of movies in casual conversation whenever possible

128. Putting two pink glazed donuts up to your eyes, and looking through them and saying "Hey I've got big pink eyes, everybody!"

129. Moonwalking

130. Telling people about how you went to watch a now well-known rock star back when they were nobodies ("So he would always be playing down at First Avenue ... you know, that was back when Prince was, like, totally, totally unknown, man. Too bad he sold out.")

131. Using a journal for your to-do lists

132. Playing Chinese checkers with a normal checker board

133. Doing it your way

134. Following your instincts

135. Listening to your heart

136. When walking by people, making a noise like "Vroom"

137. Bringing up the concept of death repeatedly in casual conversation

138. At the end of a television show saying the word "Viacom" along with the TV announcer

139. Having pizzas delivered to your friends

140. Caring about what happens to those weirdos in the Middle East

141. Doing a "double take" (Bonus: with sound effects!)

142. Pop psychology terms, like "anal" and "passive aggressive"

143. Hokey-pokey

144. Collecting figurines

145. Giving all your worldly possessions to Sun Yung Moon

146. Killing time

147. Feeding pigeons

148. Driving with your head out the window like a dog would (Bonus: doing this to dry your hair)

149. Doing a thumbs-up at something

150. Just letting go (Bonus: letting go in a relationship)

151. Letting your hair down (Bonus: you have short hair)

152. Stuffing

153. Stove-top stuffing

Dear Ma'am/Sir,

I wear a suede jacket, frequent indoor tennis courts, still keep in touch with my friends from high school,use proper-noun insults (like "No, shit, Sherlock" and "Smooth move, Ex-Lax")and ride a motorcycle because it looks cool. I feel that the best part of "Magnum, P.I." is that Rick, the guy that owns that bar, wears those power shirts (blue shirt, white collar) without a power suit, with two or three buttons undone. I think that looks cool. I'm a little worried. What if I'm cheesy? Am I cheesy?

Virginia

Aurora, Ill.

MIGHT REPLIES:

Yes, Virginia, you are cheesy. Buck up, little camper, 'cause know what? Everyone's got a little cheese in them. And that's *good*.

Dear Editors:

Please help! My mom is a cheeseball! She rolls up the windows in my convertible, answers "Right on, bucko" when I say "Don't miss me too much" and has things with cows on them all over the kitchen. It didn't used to be this way. I'm 28, moved back to her crib on the fly; my heart sinks and my stomach turns when I think "my mom is a different person." I have no one to talk to about this because my only friend keeps saying "What is 'cheeseball'?" (He's from France.) Is there anything I can do?

Forlorn in Philly

MIGHT REPLIES:

What is your problem? Of course Moms are cheesy. Shame on you. You're old enough to recognize the age-old "son-rejecting-the-mother-he's-scared-of-in-himself" thing. Quit repressing, Forlorn. Hug your mother and buy a cow apron.

installment 2
BEING HUMAN

us and them

What separates us from the animals, you ask? What is it about us humans that enables us to rule the Earth while wearing pumps and driving custom-colored Honda Civics? Higher brain processes? An incredible propensity to lie? The cotton gin? Yes, yes, and no. It's not that we daydream and muse, but that we daydream about who will attend our funeral, and muse over what it would be like to be from Mississippi. It's not the fact that we've invented places to crowd together, blow smoke in one another's faces, and pay to drink liquids that slow our brains and melt our insides. It's the fact that these places have doormen with ponytails. And it's not the fact that we stick our vile, slippery tongues into each other's mouths for fun. It's the fact that we don't usually get paid for it. It's the fact that we dress up in little, thin, soft and shiny pointed shoes to go to work. It's the way we smile when pretending that we haven't farted. It's the way we take comfort in all these things, hold them dear and valuable, and lie about really trying to make the world a better place. In this chapter, we explore the cheese that makes us who we are, the cheese by-products of our relationships and daily interactions. It is this cheese, and not simply the fact that most animals are really really stupid, that separates us from them.

Lying

To a girl/boyfriend

To your parents

To your friends

To the police

To your cellmates

Lying in the voice of that guy on "Saturday Night Live" who used to always say his girlfriend was Morgan Fairchild and who's now getting fatter and fatter and seems to be hurting for work

Lying about having seen a movie (Bonus: it's French)

Lying about having slept with someone (Bonus: they moved to, like, *Orlando*, so there's no way you can get caught!)

Lying when you really don't need to

Lying about lying

Lying about lying about lying

When forced to give up the lie, saying, "OK, you got me."

When forced to give up the lie, saying, "Oh, I was only *joking!*"

"No, no, you were great."

"What am I thinking? Oh, nothing."

"No, it's nothing."

"I love you too."

GOING OUT CHEESE
PART I

Making three different sets of plans, giving your friends the "options," and then making them pick the "best" one

Dancing in front of the mirror naked

Dancing in front of the mirror fully clothed

Dancing in front of the mirror and trying out a new dance

Walking toward the mirror to see how you look, you know, walking

Checking out the back of your hair with a hand-held mirror

Checking out your butt with a hand-held mirror

Practicing your smile

Practicing your laugh

Putting a condom in your wallet "just in case"

Bringing two condoms because "ya never know"

Wearing sexy underwear because "hey, something could happen"

Asking your friend if you have lipstick on your teeth

Asking your friend if you have anything stuck in your teeth (Bonus: your friend picks it out for you!)

154. Stove-top popcorn

155. Campfire popcorn

156. Campfire stories

157. Magazines for ferret lovers

158. While visiting Boston, *rolling* your R's as opposed to "lazying" them

159. Always thanking people in another language

160. Wearing a backpack over two shoulders

161. Wearing shoes with the word "Roos" on them

162. Saying to yourself "Oh, yeah, he/she wants me."

163. Believing in hair

164. Translating Latin

165. Translating Pig Latin

166. Raising pigs

167. Being oh-so-concerned about good health

168. Saying "please"

Being more excited about dressing up than going out

Wearing jeans and a T-shirt out

Putting on a different T-shirt and thinking it has a very different effect

PART II

Asking the cab driver to let you off a block before

Trying to scam on the bartender (Bonus: saying it was just to get free drinks)

Not realizing everyone is trying to scam on the bartender

Farting and thinking no one will notice

Ladies' Nights that are before 9:30 on a Wednesday

The "that's some damn good whiskey" wince after a doing a shot

Slamming the glass down and wiping your mouth with your sleeve

Hi-fives after shots

Having no reaction at all after doing a shot

Asking if there's a special house drink

Telling the bartender to "surprise" you

Knowing you look good (Bonus: acting like you don't know you look good)

Sending a drink to someone

Having the bartender say it

was a secret admirer

Thinking someone's giving you the eye

Giving someone the eye

Mentioning in conversation that you loooove back rubs

Guest lists

Pretending you're on a guest list when you know you're not

Ordering water

Peeing in the alley outside

Bouncers who refer to themselves as doormen

Doormen in suits

Doormen with dreadlocks (Bonus: white doormen with dreadlocks)

BEAUTY PAGEANT CHEESE	VS.	DOMINICAN REPUBLIC CHEESE
Bathing suits cut two inches below hip, worn with heels	⟷	Sweat-stained white shirt, opened to waist
Opening dance sequence in ethnic costume	⟷	Impromptu stickball games
Baton twirling in Uncle Sam outfit	⟷	Cockfights
Putting Vaseline on teeth	⟷	Sacrificing a chicken for Sante Sangre
Miss Congeniality	⟷	Pedro Guerrero
Contestant winner screams and touches face, tears brimming, crown at jaunty angle	⟵	Family of 16 living in one room shanty framed by creaky, paint-chipped fence

Having the doorman stamp the *inside* of your wrist

Hitting on cocktail waitresses (Bonus: asking "Do guys hit on you a lot?")

Ordering something "on the rocks"

Ordering something "straight up"

Ordering "top shelf"

Warning the bartender not to give you any of that "cheap stuff"

Barbacks with multiple piercings and a bar towel tucked into the back of their pants

Tipping a quarter

Pitchers

Women who drink light beer

Men who drink light beer

Men and women who drink light beer together

Bonding with the bartender

Calling a woman bartender a "bartendress"

Telling the bartender it's your birthday and expecting a free drink (Bonus: it's not *really* your birthday, ha ha!)

Telling the bartender to make your drink "extra strong" (Bonus: winking afterward)

Pounding shots (Bonus: *slamming* shots)

Telling what happened the last time you "did shots" just before you "pound" or "slam" one

Lemon drops

Black and Tans

Sex on the Beach

Flaming drinks

White wine spritzers

Offering to buy "the next round"

Not buying the next round

Bar time (Bonus: telling everyone that, like, bar time is *always* 15 minutes ahead)

Begging for a drink after last call

Security guys with Mag lights

Being a regular

Eating bar fruit

PICK UP CHEESE

Asking the bartender for a pen

Lying about your job

Lying about your age

Giving a fake phone number

Giving a fake name

Memorizing a phone number because you don't have a pen

169. Lollygagging

170. Reading the Bible

171. Believing in the Bible

172. Believing that Kurt Loder and Tabitha Soren are speaking directly to you

173. Saying "Well, you know what *that* means" to anything (Bonus: about someone with large feet)

174. Hanging pencils out of your nostrils

175. Singing along to a song on the radio

176. Singing along to a newscast on the radio

177. Sorority pillow fights

178. Fraternity pillow fights

179. Living to eat, not eating to live

180. Saluting

181. Saluting and clicking your heels together

182. Seeing how long you can balance something on your finger

MUSING CHEESE *You're all alone, just thinking, just pondering, just daydreaming, but there is still cheese...*

Musing about being famous

Musing about having a better body

Musing about giving it all up and moving to a little cottage in Vermont

Musing about giving it all up and living on a tropical island

Musing about being able to summon nature's creatures to aid in your fight against evil

Musing about being a stuntperson

Daydreaming about how if Courteney Cox only had a chance to get to know you she'd totally fall in love with a nice guy like you

Musing about the people you've dated

Counting in your head the people you've slept with (Bonus: in order!)

Wondering how fat people have sex

Musing about the whereabouts of Tina Yothers

Considering changing your name to something more patriotic

Considering changing your name to something that rhymes

Musing about plastic surgery

Musing about plastic surgery for your friends

Musing about plastic surgery for total strangers

Trying to move objects with your mind

Pretending you're in a movie

Pretending you're in a video

Choosing who you'd like to have a child with based solely on their good genes

Wondering if retarded people are really geniuses

Wishing you never quit piano

Believing it's never too late to start a band

Getting a joke once you get home

Thinking of what you should have said but didn't

Wishing you could go back in time to say what you should have said but didn't

Musing on your high school senior quote

Wishing you had written a different, wittier senior quote

Finding quotes that you wish you'd found when you were a senior (Bonus: they're by Ralph Waldo Emerson!)

Believing that if you were a Roman in Roman times you would not have thought watching the Christians being thrown to the lions was entertaining

Believing that had you been a rich, white plantation owner, way back when, you wouldn't have slaves; and even if you did, you would have been really, really nice to them

Thinking you're going to die young

Imagining what people would do if they found out you died

Thinking about what you want done when you die (Bonus: telling someone and making them *promise* to do it)

Giving your best friend's phone number and pretending it's yours

Giving someone your card

Sending someone a drink and winking at them when they get it

Dancing and drinking at the same time

Dancing and making small talk at the same time

Dancing and singing at the same time

Going up to someone on a bet

Saying "Really, I never do this…"

Saying "This band's great!"

Saying "This band sucks!"

Saying "You know, I used to play in a band" (Bonus: you're not lying!)

SEX CHEESE

Calling someone up at 3 a.m. and asking him or her to "come over" (Bonus: pleading by saying, "Aw c'mon, just come over") (Double Bonus: being the stupid horny idiot who actually "comes over")

The walk of shame

183. Crisco massages

184. Getting drunk

185. Red wine that's "best when chilled"

186. Pronouncing discount store names with elite sounding French names (Targét, K mart, etc.)

187. Saving your toenails for a special "love broth"

188. Making the sound of the Six Million-Dollar Man when you run or jump

189. Making the Chevy Chase Putting Sound

190. Talking like a sportscaster

191. Talking like a sportscaster, and narrating yourself winning The Big Game

192. Flying pigs

193. Playing poker

194. Playing strip poker with someone you like and it's just the two of you

---

YOU GOT CHOCOLATE IN MY PEANUT BUTTER LIST #1

What to put in an empty ashtray cheese/ Waiting in line cheese

Whistling

Tapping your foot

Foreign coins

Shoving your hands in your pockets and leaning back and forth

Potpourri

Saying "Some line, huh? Yessirree."

Torn up pieces of paper

Matches from around the world

Having your ticket out

Change for the bus

Jangling change for the bus in your pocket

Bringing a magazine

Bringing a friend

Bringing a chair

Bringing all of the above, and food

Giving disapproving looks to people who cut

Jelly beans

THE "WHOO! PARTY! FRIENDS FOREVER! LOOK AT MY BEER!"

THE "OH YEAH, I'M LOOKING PREEEETTY GOOD" TWO-HANDED COMB

THE "YEAH, LIKE I REALLY CARE" FAUX JERK-OFF MOTION

THE "HEEEY, RIGHT BACK ATCHA!"

Walking home with your underwear in your pocket

Trying to sneak out of a bedroom in the morning without the other person hearing

Hand lotion (Bonus: Jergens)

Having a handy place you keep the Jergens

K-Y Jelly (Bonus: calling it "K-Y")

Colored condoms, you know, just for fun

French ticklers

Vibrators (Bonus: *black* vibrators!)

Testicles (Bonus: calling them nuts, balls, cajones or the family jewels)

Anal beads

Ben Wa Balls

Crotchless panties

Crotchless panties with garters

Sex in a limo

Sex in an elevator

Videotaping yourself having sex (Bonus: in an elevator!)

Ordering pay-per-view porn

SALON CHEESE

Going for a free consultation

Getting a free haircut from a beauty school

Hair salons with pun names ("Hair It Is," "Hair Razor's")

Light conversation with your hairdresser

Calling him/her your "stylist"

Picking a hairstyle out of one of the magazines and wanting your hair just like that

Drawing a picture of the hairstyle you want and showing it to your stylist

Naming a hairstyle after a person (Bonus: the Dorothy Hamill)

Colorists

Buying products available "only in salons"

Hairdressers who say "We" ("First we will angle the back and then graduate the sides with subtle layering so we can show our natural highlights.")

Saying "I trust you" to your hairdresser

Moaning while you get your hair washed

The blue liquid-filled jar that sanitizes combs

Back waxing

195. Licking the bowl

196. Feeling superior

197. Having a shower "routine"

198. Double-tying your shoelaces

199. Peeping through keyholes

200. When walking up stairs, skipping every other stair

201. When walking up stairs, skipping every two stairs

202. When walking up stairs, skipping every three stairs

203. When walking up stairs and skipping stairs, losing your balance and falling

204. Pulling backward on a revolving door so that the person in the door gets trapped

205. Pulling backward on a revolving door so that the person in the door gets trapped so that your mob buddies can mow them down in a hail of gunfire

29

BEING A MOM CHEESE

Asking you if you have enough money to eat

Gardening tools

Gardening gloves

Seasoned olive oil

Wishing you luck before finals (Bonus: you're in law school)

Wishing you luck before you finalize a multimillion-dollar business venture

Brooches

Foreign exchange students

Swearing

Wearing jeans

Riding bikes (Bonus: trying to get Dad to ride tandem)

Trying to get Dad to take her out on the town

The Mom Cut

Talking about herself in a sexual way

Saying "Oh, lighten up"

Saying "You used to be so cute"

Saying "You've got something on your seat," referring to your butt

Putting on lipstick for church

Wearing fur

Clipping articles and sending them to you, F.Y.I.

Claiming to be able to get an erection "when the wind blows"

Getting an erection when the wind blows

Finding tattoos

Making excuses to go to sleep right after you have sex (Bonus: saying it's because the other person is so good they "tired you out")

Actually trying to think of mundane, asexual things like nuns or cats or the original cast of "Cop Rock" in order to pro- long sex (Bonus: actually knowing the original cast of "Cop Rock" and still coming too soon)

Sex with your eyes open

Sex with your eyes closed

Sex with the lights on

Sex with the lights off

Turning on the TV and shutting off the lights, because hey, that's pretty good lighting for sex

Putting on music for sex (Bonus: Sade) (Double Bonus: Ravel) (Triple Kitty Bonus: The Orb!)

That special half-hidden place you keep condoms, that's within arm's reach of your bed but not soooo noticeable

Saying "that was great" (Bonus: lying)

Asking someone if they came (Bonus: answering with a lie) (Double Bonus: you're a guy!)

Changing into lingerie before

Having a smoke after

One person is making noises, the other isn't

Saying "I want you" (Bonus: pausing, then adding, "sooo much")

Covering up when you walk to the bathroom

Sucking toes

Biting

Being tied up but know- ing you can get out

Being tied up and not getting out

Breaking the bed

Planning when you'll have sex (Bonus: penciling it in your daily planner)

Talking it over the day before (Bonus: you factor in being tired at work the next day)

Planning when you'll masturbate

Having sex in your parent's bed

"Making love"

Makin' it

Doing the nasty

Knockin' boots

Gettin' down

Referring to genitalia in the third person

"Do you want to?"

Fantasizing about someone else

Trying to figure out who it is you're having sex with

Licking lips

Hickeys

Whispering

Masturbating with household appliances

Vacuum cleaners

Putting on candles and jazz while the other person's in the bathroom (Bonus: you don't even acknowledge it when they come back)

Afterward: they tell you to lock the door and slip the key under it

FUNNY PERSON IN PUBLIC CHEESE

You're a funny person in public! When there are lots of people around, you're the go-to guy when it comes to humor! Following are situations in public, followed by what you, as the Funny Person in Public, do.

SITUATION	YOUR REACTION	RESULT
You're in a large crowd, moving slowly together toward an entrance/exit	"Moo!"	Big laughs
You're at a concert, and the band has asked for requests	"Freebird!"	Big laughs
The movie's over, the credits are rolling	"See? There I am—key grip!"	Big laughs
You're at an art museum looking at something abstract	"This sucks! My kid brother could do that!"	Big laughs
You're a pedestrian crossing the street, and a car turns in front of you	You hit the trunk, yell "Ow! You hit me!" and limp away holding your leg	Big laughs

206. Black light fun

207. Making the sound of Jaws when you're swimming

208. Making the sound of Jaws III when you're swimming

209. Throwing a gallon of bleach in a fish hatchery

210. Sniping

211. Hunting for snipe

212. Initiation rituals in general

213. Bathtub masturbation

214. Playing cat's cradle

215. Tacos

216. Not referring to espresso sizes as small, medium and large but instead as short, tall and grande

217. Spitting on your hands and then rubbing them together (Bonus: before chopping wood!)

218. Magnifying glass fun

219. Pointing and winking at famous people you don't know just to impress your model date

cheese unique to we gals

For all that can be debated about being a woman, there is one truism: Women have a style to their cheese that is unrivaled. Call it attention to details, female intuition, a certain "Je ne sais quoi," but women know how to scent their underwear drawer, know the personality of a passerby based on their clothing and know what they want out of Valentine's Day. So call yourself Sally, Mertle or Jo, be a poet, a housewife or a construction worker, act the part or fight your role, but if you are a woman, admit that you like to feel powder fresh—at least every once in a while.

Scented tampons

Debating o.b. versus Tampax

Debating tampons versus pads (Bonus: expressing disbelief when someone argues for pads)

Feminine deodorant commercials

That "not so fresh" feeling

Douche jokes

Control top pantyhose

Putting nail polish on a run

Knowing the names of all the supermodels

Referring to models by their first names only

Talking about your boobs

Asking your boyfriend if he thinks you're fat (Bonus: not believing him when he says no)

Blowing the dust off your diaphragm

IUDs

Treasure trails

Going on a date for a free meal

Bachelorette parties

Bachelorette parties at Chippendale's

DIET CHEESE	VS.	"TOWERING INFERNO" CHEESE
Eyes are bigger than stomach	⟷	100-story building catches on fire
Appetite suppressants that are chocolate-covered caramels	⟷	Elevator cord breaks, dropping thousands of feet at breakneck speed
Drinking 6 to 8 glasses of water a day	⟷	Paul Newman feels the office door. It feels hot
Six ounces of water-packed tuna on dry whole wheat toast, one cup plain nonfat yogurt, black coffee	⟷	Man engulfed in flames breaks through glass door, takes seven steps, falls to ground, writhing in agony

Bachelorette parties at Chippendale's and you give your number to the "construction worker"

Forgetting to take the Pill and then doubling up the next day

Talking to your girlfriend while in adjoining stalls

Talking to your girlfriend while you put on lipstick and she's still peeing

Saying, "Shit, I got my fucking period!"

Euphemisms for your period

Plucking your eyebrows and then using an eyebrow pencil

Plucking your breast hairs

Shaving before sex

Dying your hair blond (Bonus: you're dishwater blond already!)

Highlights, y'know, for something different

Playing on stereotypes associated with your new hair color (e.g., dye it red and think of yourself as a fiery redhead)

Scrunching

Feeling powder fresh

Feeling like a spring breeze

Feeling petal soft

Rose water

Really liking flowers

Giving someone your number because you feel bad telling them you don't want them to call you

Being one of those women who always has more guy friends

Hanging out with gay guys because they'll go out dancing

Applauding Madonna as a feminist

Big key chains

Asking for directions

Earring racks

Herb and fruit shower gel

Printed toiletry bags instead of plain ones

Traveling light

Pulling hair during fights with other women

Silk scarves

Girls' night out

Going Dutch

Being a tomboy

Jean patches

Sexy ski pants

Nature tattoos (Bonus: a butterfly!)

Hot pink gel bottles (instead of white or blue)

Home Ec

220. Not wearing underwear

221. Conserving water

222. Playing a new album and reading the lyrics along with the singer

223. Coleslaw

224. Air bags

225. James Garner

226. Shower sex

227. Giving the cashier proper change

228. Playing with blue-screen technology

229. Patting your head while swirling your belly

230. A cappella singing

231. Bonsai trees

232. Colonics

233. Believing in love

234. Handcuff fun

235. Amateur rocketry

236. Wearing "I'm with Stupid" T-shirts

237. Learning

238. Gary Powers

CHEESE: THE CONVERSATION

Cookie dough

Pedicures

Choosing a house to "get ready" at

Planning outfits (Bonus: days in advance!)

Braiding each other's hair

Feeling like you owe the slob something because he bought you dinner

Stretch marks

Iron-poor blood

Bikini waxes

Pink, fluffy bedspreads (Bonus: for a canopy bed!)

Crash dieting for Spring Break (Bonus: in Daytona!)

Having a signature scent

Female laxatives

Quiet time

Filling up on rice cakes

Slim-Fast and pizza

Diet Coke and Oreos

MALE CHEESE
See Sports (p.120)

BEING SICK CHEESE

Regis & Kathie Lee

Chicken soup

Getting drunk on NyQuil

Making jokes about rectal thermometers, ha-ha

Eating children's aspirins because they're chewable and taste like Tang

Bathrobes

Slippers

Getting someone to wait on you, just like Mom used to do

That kind of tissue with moisturizing lotion on it

Talking about how sick you are in your affected sick voice

Answering the phone in your affected sick voice

Limiting yourself to a diet of breakfast foods

Feeling like ass

Feeling like hell

Feeling like death (Bonus: warmed over)

Bed lice

Bed sores

Boils

Rashes

Leeches

Night sweats

Slow, painful death

239. Responding to the statement "Gimme a break" with "Arm or leg?"

240. Referring to Europeans by seldom-used archaic nicknames: Limey, Kraut, Frog, etc.

241. Trying to get people to ask something about you by asking the same of them, especially when you know you have a better answer

242. When passing gas, lifting a leg (á la a dog peeing), then finishing up with a sigh of, presumably, relief

243. "It smells like ass in here"

244. "Who dropped ass in here?"

245. Dropping trou'

246. When pregnant, eating for two

247. Double-bass drum kits

248. White cars

249. White boots

250. White appliances

251. Upon turning 13, wishing you were Jewish

gym cheese

Mirrors

Mirrors everywhere

Pretending that you have to look in the mirror the whole time—to make sure you're doing the exercise right

Having a workout partner

Having a personal trainer

Grunting and shouting when lifting weights

Grunting and shouting when spotting someone who's lifting weights

Sweating on the equipment (Bonus: not wiping it up!)

Power shakes

Carboloading

Rehydrating

Oiling up

Posing down

Spritzing water on your face with your fingers (Bonus: looking in the mirror—you look sexy!)

Walking around with a water bottle (Bonus: it holds like 3 gallons!)

Matching head, wrist, and ankle sweat bands

Hanging out in the locker room for long periods of time, naked

Falling off the treadmill

Social events sponsored by your gym

Getting in touch with your body

Wearing a leotard outside the gym

Wearing your towel around your neck

Referring to workout clothes as "gym togs"

Stretching so everyone can watch you

Being friends with the people who work in the gift shop, reception area, and towel sign-out areas

Water aerobics

Putting on makeup first

Swapping stats

Aerobics instructors who wear head sets

Knowing your measurements

RIDING THE BUS CHEESE	VS.	BEING DEAD CHEESE
Falling down when the bus starts	⬌	Jumping around on clouds
Telling dirty jokes to the driver	⬌	Telling dirty jokes to saints
Singing along to the cool song on your Walkman	⬌	Wearing your wings real low
Reading the ads	⬌	Accessorizing your toga-robe thing
Making announcements to the whole bus	⬌	Making jokes about people in Hell

Feeling "the burn"

Getting the negative

Jazzy warm-ups

Relaxing cool-downs

Wearing ankle weights to the grocery store

Padded workout bras

Spitting on your hands before lifting

Spitting on someone else before lifting

All-white workout outfits

Giving yourself a little pep talk before lifting (Bonus: doing it out loud)

Checking your heart rate (Bonus: with your digital watch!)

12 1/2 lb. weights

Slamming down your weights

"Can I work in with you?"

"You done with that?"

"So, whatchu benchin' these days?"

"Oh yeah? Pussy."

CLARIFICATION

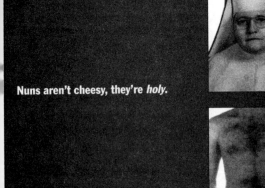

Nuns aren't cheesy, they're *holy*.

Nudes aren't cheesy, they're *dirty*.

252. Chianti

253. "I'm a poet and I just don't know it!"

254. Saying "This song rocks," and then turning the volume up

255. Turning up the volume in your hair

256. Pumping up the jams

257. Making fun of people you envy

258. Envying people you make fun of

259. Offering an "insider's" view on things

260. Smoking it if you got it

261. Clear Band-Aids

262. The double-edged sword

263. Speaking with a faux British accent, especially after having watched a British film

264. "You sold me!"

265. Having a partner

266. "I sure don't"

gay cheese

Hairdressers, aerobics instructors, fashion designers. Interior decorators, gallery owners, and yes, that well-dressed fella in your office. These are the people we turn to when we want to look good, when we accessorize, choose a new hairstyle or pick out fabric for the sofa. So, you wonder, gay cheese: is it possible? Or is it one of those witty oxymorons, like "military intelligence" or "good-looking Canadian"?

Sure, many gays are stylish, but there are others. So be careful. You might mistake the following artifacts of gay culture for hip—but trust us, fromage through and through. And as gays become mainstreamed and the mainstream gets a little funny, there's surely more to come.

Referring to other gay men with female pronouns

Dressing like a woman, but feeling like a man

Dressing like a woman, and acting like a bossy socialite, a forlorn starlet or a cliché fag

Dressing up as Patsy Cline

Showing your shaved legs

Reenacting a Scarlett/Rhett kiss

Talking like a black woman (Bonus: saying "Don't even go there, girlfriend!")

Caesars

Calvins

Speedos

Suntans

Biceps

Nude beaches

New Order

Chaps

Lamb chops

Girlfriends

Houseplants

Double income, no kids

Long white gloves

Red ribbon tattoos

Faghag bashing

Believing everyone's gay too

Coming out anthologies

Coming out on Oprah

Rumors about "gay" celebrities

Straight celebrities who are "gay friendly"

Gay magazine covers featuring straight celebs who are "gay friendly"

Sigfried & Roy

Bob & Rod Jackson-Paris

Elton John

The Elton John AIDS Foundation

The web site for the Elton John AIDS Foundation

The Gay Gene

Gay jeans (you know, 501s)

Cruising the park

Cruising the personal ads

Cruising the Web

Nature vs. nurture debate

Babs vs. Judy debate

Daddies

Overbearing mothers

Heather Has Two Mommies

Dinah Shore

The Dinah Shore weekend

Dykes on Bikes

Women-only spaces

Keith Haring calendars

Gay neighbors (or roommates or best friends)

Gay neighbors (or roommates or best friends) on sitcoms

They're always so *nice!*

Rainbow-laden, gay pride paraphernalia

Using gay pride to sell stuff to the gay market (e.g., Rainbow Java)

Ribbed T-shirts

"Straight Not Narrow" tees

Straight-acting gays

Gay-acting straights

Gay comedians

Gay nights at straight clubs

Gay jokes told with a lisp, ha ha

Movies in which an actor who once played a Star Trek commander plays a flamboyant gay decorator

Marky Mark

The Funky Bunch

Air force cheese/Doing some work around the house on the weekend cheese

Jumpsuits

Mirrored sunglasses

Mustaches

Caulk

Landing gear

Nicknames like "Ace"

Thinking about being the Red Baron

Thinking about being Tom Cruise

Thinking about being Tom Skerrit

Drywall

Talking like Chuck Yeager

Bombing stuff

Storm windows

Spackle

---

267. Gettin' some lovin'

268. "Don't even go there"

269. "Don't take me there"

270. Élan, verve and Je ne sais quoi

271. Canadians

272. The French

273. French Canadians

274. Birkenstocks

275. Calling old boy/girlfriends when you're drunk

276. Gore Vidal

277. Call Gore Vidal when you're drunk

278. "Modern rock"

279. Teaching parrots cuss words

280. Putting stuff in folders

281. Phoning first

282. Being thoughtful

283. Teamwork

284. Leading a horse to water

installment 3
BRAVE NEW WORLD ORDER

cheese of our busy, bustling, sexy new lives

What great visionary could have foreseen a brighter future? Years ago, people were poor and sad. But now there are computers in every pot and cars that talk when you open their doors. There are electronic town meetings, friendly multinational corporations and the thrill of using the Dewey Decimal System. Where were we when all this happened? Maybe we were trying to figure out childproof lighters or just what in the hell Strom Thurmond was saying, or maybe we were all sleeping the soft and dreamy sleep of a more simple time. A time when men were men and people cried out for the likes of Herbert Hoover. Those certainly were the days. But alas, they are no more. Today our world seems to spin with an ever more ferocious speed, and not even Superman flying at his fastest in the other direction could make a difference. Still, we try. We wrap our gifts in recyclable wrapping paper and are nice to homeless people. We listen to the pundits and prognosticators and clamor about the issues. We think about how cool things will be when commercials on the Internet come true. We think vague thoughts about "telecommuting." And we try to know a thing or two about wine. Still, just like Juice Newton used to say—and we're paraphrasing here—"Time marches on, but my career, well, that's another story."

CORPORATE CHEESE

Happy hour

Kitchenettes

Colored paper clips

Personalized memo pads

Company volleyball games (Bonus: against your rivals!)

Anonymous, bitter notes about leaving the kitchenette dirty, eating someone else's food or no one ever buying soap

Talking about people "going postal"

Changing into heels when you get to the office

Biking to work (Bonus: wearing rubber bands around your cuffs so they don't get stuck in the ol' chain)

Answering your home phone as if it's work

Feet on the desk, crossed

Talking on the phone with one foot up on the chair, leaning on your knee

Walking around a restaurant on a cell phone, trying to find the right spot for a good connection

Office temp/bike messenger romances

Shoulder pads

"Brown-bagging it"

"Brown bag" lunch meetings

Brown-nosing during brown bag lunch meetings

Getting your photo in the company newsletter, then distributing copies to friends and relatives

The "there's more to me than this suit" earring

The "I still have my beliefs" lapel pin and/or campaign button

Trying to win hipster points with the bike messengers ("Hey, didja see that Meat Puppets concert? Fwah!")

Donuts on Friday!

Employee discount clubs

Getting elected office Fire Warden (Bonus: wearing the orange vest)

"Per your request"

Golf balls with the corporate logo

Lucite service awards

Arguing that "corporate culture" is an oxymoron

Telling long, exasperated stories about what a long, hard commute you had

Office parks

Football pools

Garbage basket hoops

"Synergy"

285. Giving back cuts in line

286. Mickey Mouse clothing (Bonus: Mickey Mouse clothing on men)

287. Responding "thank *you*" to a thank you

288. "Doin'" anything

289. Boppin' 'til you drop

290. Referring to your house as your "domain"

291. Referring to your apartment as your "crib"

292. Referring to your apartment as your "place of residence"

293. Scamming the post office by reversing the "to" and "from" addresses and not adding postage

294. "So, where do you see yourself in five years?"

295. When cereal talks to you

Temps who boast of their plans for office supply theft and other petty forms of sabotage

Arriving at work an hour earlier than anyone to look like a real go-getter

Getting permission to play music

Passing out business cards to people at social engagements

Placing unwanted documents in the "circular file"

Bulletproof limos

Putting people on hold just for the fun of it

Photocopier fun

Crank calling your receptionist

Having a company masseuse

Having a company "masseuse"

"Having" the company "masseuse"

Overusing quotation marks

Bailey's in the coffee

Ring around the collar

Status meetings

Chain of command

Expense account abuse

Squirt gun wars

Getting psyched for the big office party, where you're really gonna cut loose

Retreats

CONFERENCE ROOM FUN

Bodily noises

Gagging and making a motion to everyone like it's the person sitting next to you

When someone laughs at a question you pose, you say, "I was speaking hypothetically, Shitmouth."

In the middle of a meeting declaring a "point of procedure"

The business card handout to everyone (Bonus: doing it like a Vegas blackjack dealer!)

After the business card handout, saying "Ante up!" (Huge laughs)

Telling your client that you had donuts for them but the "office squirrels" ate them right before the meeting

Spinning in your chair

Spinning in your chair till it stops and then asking the person next to you to keep it spinning

Telling the group an off-color joke

Tittering after the president offers a comment on something

When someone brings up a very tangential point you stand up and applaud

Pretending to take notes, drawing superheroes instead

Rolling your eyes

Crossing your eyes

Saying, "If I may interject, here …"

Saying, "Can I raise a practical question at this point?"

Saying, "Hmmm, interesting …"

Saying, "OK, let's get back to the subject at hand."

Saying to the person speaking, "You're trying to ruin me, aren't you?"

Making conference calls from the conference room

Crying

Patting coworkers on the back as you walk out

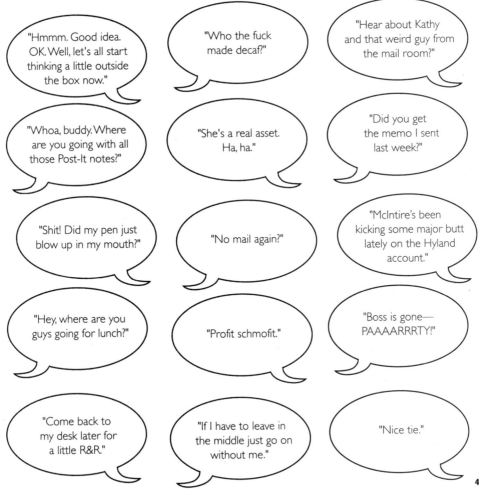

45

THE "I REALLY ENJOYED LUNCH, SUE"
THREE-HANDED HANDSHAKE AND
MEANINGFUL LOOK

THE "I'LL JUST KILL MYSELF IF I GET
ANOTHER MEMO/I CAN'T WAIT UNTIL FRIDAY
WHEN I CAN START MY *REAL* LIFE"
PULLING-OUT-THE-HAIR MOVE

THE SATISFIED BUSINESSMAN ON THE
PLANE AFTER THE BIG DEAL SATISFIED
SMILE & BIG STRETCH MANEUVER

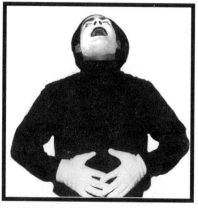

THE "I OWN YOU ALL AND COULD RUIN
EVERY LAST ONE OF YOU LITTLE WORKER
MAGGOTS" MANIACAL BELLYLAUGH

The I-don't-know-what-to-say-to-you-because-I've-already-said-good-morning smile & wink

Catching sight of a coworker's cleavage and then forgetting what you were saying

Overuse of pointing sticks

Misfiling things for fun

Taking your own, personal home supplies to work for office use

Baking something nice for the whole office

Letting things like profits and losses get in the way of a good time

Sneaking up on and scaring the cleaning crew

Pouring gin in the office water cooler

Getting toner on your hands, telling your boss it's the black plague, and going home

After a few months at the job, realizing that 4:30 p.m. has become a "special occasion"

Pirating software

Playing computer games

Bossing people around

Posting fake inner-office job opportunities on the bulletin board to find out who really doesn't like their job, and then firing them

Holiday gift exchanges

Having company spirit

Believing that the corporation really cares about you

Taking the office's fresh flowers home to the wife

Having a drawer full of starched white shirts just in case

Massacring Kinko's at the corporate softball tourney

Having health insurance

Sending fake letters of resignation to your supervisor as a joke

Telephone headrests

Wondering what the "k" in 401(k) stands for

Telling people that you're way too busy for fire drills

Trade shows

BRIEFCASE CHEESE

Combinations
Combinations that are your name
Combinations that are "666"
Bulletproof
Full of hundreds
Full of Krugerrands
Full of bullion
Full of bouillon cubes

296. Bringing in a ringer

297. Bringing in a winner

298. Using numbers as verbs (e.g., "He's 86ed from the club" or "We 69ed")

299. 69ing

300. Fate

301. Using a 24-hour clock

302. Having college friends nicknamed Murph, Mobes, or Scully

303. Mixed drinks involving sexual innuendos

304. Second-best friends

305. Hitting a friend's bumper while driving behind them, ha-ha

306. Fountains

307. Room service

308. Big noses

309. Sherman tanks

310. Dreaming that you can fly

311. Flashing people

312. Milking cows

313. Badges

advertising cheese

The sweat, the shoes, the wet pavement, the shoes, the attitude, the shoes. Just Do It. Each word, by itself, meaning nothing. Together, still meaning nothing. And yet somehow meaning everything. Now, it seems like we're all Just Doing It. Doing it all the time—on the court, at the office, in the car, at church. And does it stop there? Hell no! We've got problems. And thank sweet Jesus that our hardworking and well-dressed friends at the world's ad agencies are there to help. Think about it: Would we have thought to wear Easy Spirit high heels on the basketball court? Now, with those extra two inches, a lot of white people can dunk. Coke? Sure, who hasn't ridden that wave one time or another? Be young, have fun!

Commercials with monks in them

Commercials with monks in them where, even though the monks are supposed to not ever talk or everything, they just *have* to say something about the extraordinary product they've just enjoyed

Choosy moms

Dentists who just can't agree

Happy people

Hugging

Race car driver/pilot takes off his helmet and—surprise—it's a beautiful woman!

Commercials for makeup that show models being photographed

Commericals for sweaters that feature snowshoes and/or wood-chopping

Using computer animation to show how acne products work

Using computer animation to show how hair is strengthened by shampoo

Comparison tests (Bonus: the participants are blindfolded!)

Using life transitions to sell cars

Any commercial that uses James Brown's "I feel good" song when someone tries the product

Any commercial that uses those catchy, familiar and meaningful songs from *The Big Chill*

Non-dysfunctional families

The Club (Police say "use" it)

Sears' valiant efforts to market high-fashion clothing

Poor Jaclyn Smith

Women who twirl for the camera

Having it your way, right away

Instant-coffee romances

Commercials featuring a real-life celebrity couple being coy and combative with each other

Old men spouting sage wisdom on a bench in front of a small-town store

Singing bologna songs while fishing

Girls with curly hair

Classical music for expensive car commercials, country for trucks spots, and guitar-solo rock for sports cars

Commercials for TV shows

Commercials for TV networks

Commercials for TV networks featuring all the stars from their TV shows singing and jumping and all kinds of shit like that

Commercials set to the tune of "Disco Inferno"

Treating women like the ignorant car-buying fools they really are

Dramatizations (Bonus: of someone sneezing)

Any product that begins with "The Sounds of …"

Portraying children as being smarter than adults—the little rascals!

Adhering to claymation even though we have computers now

Commercials to make you feel a part of a generation—giving you an "us and them" feeling

Covered wagons

Using all three dimensions in outdoor advertising

Microsoft referring to its products as "stuff" for the benefit of those of us who don't understand all that computer magic

White teeth

Hotels that leave a light on for you

Ads from a pet's perspective

Those crazy kids dropping and spilling and spreading food all over your hi-tech carpet

Children sucking up to or battling with sports figures for soda, or fast food

Sponsoring arcane sports stats breaks (The McDonald's Free Throw Percentage Roundup, The Napa Auto Parts' Two-Minute Warning)

Words floating around people

Young college grads playing football in the cold and mud

Commercials for U.S. states (Bonus: Tennessee's "We're playing your song")

Camera companies that play on our desire to be rebellious

People acting like they have just way too much energy in general

Beers that make it snow

People running while their voiceovers talk to us

Indians crying over litter

Using liquid soap to write words on tough grass stains

Talking foods in the refrigerator

Trying to pass off instant coffee

Loving, and showing how much you love, to fly

Baking elves, elves who bake

Flannel-wearing hardware pimps

314. Merit badges

315. Walking while playing a guitar

316. Hitchhiking with a guitar

317. Electrical outlet fun

318. Putting your pinkie out while drinking tea

319. Self-reflection

320. Reflecting pools

321. Rorschach tests

322. Rag wool socks

323. Septic tank fun

324. Black watch plaid

325. Tartan plaid

326. Getting rid of a fever by submersing yourself in a bathtub full of ice water

327. Referring to inanimate objects by baby names (water = wa wa, blanket = blankie)

328. Remarking on women's facial hair

329. Death by hara-kiri

330. Death by Harry Caray

331. Big hats

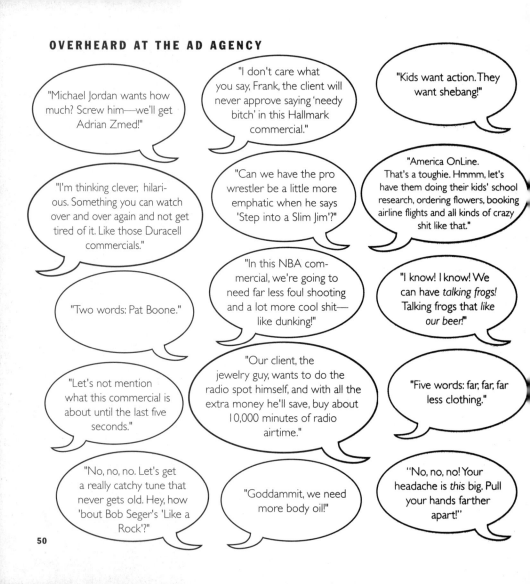

50

Cologne ads with whispering

Gratuitous use of the surf

Words used on the screen but they speak anyway so it's kind of like a read-along

Cats with moving mouths

The table polish vs. wax dilemma

Showing the underside of a Stridex pad after you wipe your face

Loving what Toyota does for you

Those minds from Minolta

Finding the beef

Deserving a break today

Zamfir

Bored dishwasher repairmen

Fast cars

Hot women

Fast cars and hot women and other crazy shit

Emphasizing the practicality of minivans, like you wouldn't buy one to pick up the babes

Cars that can jump over other cars given a ramp and a whole lotta speed

Trucks that can carry other trucks, implying that the truck on top can't carry the truck on the bottom

Engineers in white lab coats

Engineers in white lab coats with clipboards making notes while standing on a race track

Corinthian leather

Believing that there is such a thing as Corinthian leather

Being both the president and a client of the company

Ads for the local TV news that, in the time it takes to tease us about the big story, could have communicated the gist of it if they cared at all about informing us

Cars that can pop wheelies

Topical weed killer solutions

Respecting German engineering

Mop demonstrations

Vacuums that can cut your hair

Correspondence courses

Correspondence courses endorsed by celebrities who didn't take the courses themselves

Max Headroom

Those strangely pedaphilic Dutch Boy commercials

Man-on-the-street-in-Buffalo testimonials for sinus and cold relief

Substituting blue liquid for baby pee in diaper ads

Any Subway ad

332. Thinking up truly innovative ways to pull a tooth

333. Candy samplers

334. Wearing a belt and suspenders at the same time

335. Wearing a belt and suspenders and leather nipple clamps at the same time

336. Believing that celebrities are just real people like you and me

337. Butt beads

338. Wearing butt beads as a necklace

339. Abusing prescription drugs

340. Referring to NAS-DAQ as "Nazdack"

341. Calling up a stockbroker at random and, without identifying yourself, screaming into the telephone: "SELL! YOU MOTHERFUCKER, SELL IT ALL OR I'LL HAVE YOUR ASS!" and then hanging up

That Kool-Aid pitcher guy who always breaks through walls, and doesn't care a lick about structural damage

Getting fooled by the Parkay

Women who sing and smile in orange juice commercials

Any very colorful and fruity Skittles campaign

When you bite into some candy and there's like some crazy flavor monsoon that presumably wipes out the whole tropical village where you're at, but what the hay, it tastes great

Rolling a Rolo to your pal

Crying over a Hallmark ad

Cigarette companies that spell "cool" with a K

Implying that cute little frogs and ants drink beer

Strangely provocative milk moustaches on All-America role-model types

Trying to get between Brooke and her Calvins

Football fanatics that want to go to the Superbowl—or, if not there, then definitely McDonald's

Ad series, where you get to know and love a certain recurring character

Realizing that he's a Pepper,

she's a Pepper and wanting to be a Pepper, too

MORE OVERHEARD:

"Tagging our own billboards? So post-modern. I like it."

"The music for this beer commerical? I've got three words: Good time rock 'n' roll!"

METEOR CRASHING INTO THE EARTH CHEESE	VS.	THINGS TO DO IF YOU'RE CANADIAN CHEESE
Anticipation of meteor becomes global event	⟷	Insisting on singing your particular little national anthem at hockey games
Meteor is actually spaceship full of aliens who get out and turn everything to dust	⟷	Instead of having stars or eagles or stripes on your flag, having a leaf
The only survivors appear to be extremely well-developed teenagers	⟷	Having a whole huge part of your country that's pretty much too cold to live in and no one can remember the name of
Survivors find time for romance	⟷	Trying to secede
Survivors determined to find other signs of life	⟷	Winnipeg

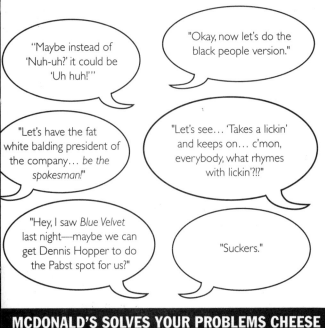

MCDONALD'S SOLVES YOUR PROBLEMS CHEESE

PROBLEM	SOLUTION
Little League team loses	Go to McDonald's
Team wins championship	Go to McDonald's
Can't think of a place to go on a first date	Go to McDonald's
50th anniversary	Go to McDonald's
Hungry?	Go to McDonald's

342. **Mailing a letter to yourself**

343. **Mailing a letter to yourself and then acting like you don't know what it is when you open it**

344. **Actually reading the letter that you sent to yourself**

345. **Believing that the letter is a love letter from a famous model**

346. **Not responding to that model who keeps writing letters to you**

347. **Pulling out the tablecloth from underneath a set table**

348. **Confections**

349. **Believing that there's more to life than fancy book learnin'**

350. **Attending the University of Hard Knocks**

351. **Frescoes**

352. **Frescas**

353. **Frisco**

techno cheese

The thing about this complex, contemporary world of ours is, it's so modern. It's even more modern than we thought it would be, even more modern than Stanley Kubrick and Arthur C. Clarke thought. For starters, much brighter and sleeker. There are way more buttons and blips and amplifiers and track pads and silvery things than even those guys thought possible. And everyone just fucking loves it. I mean, it's not as great as the Jetsons, but then again, I think we're all having a pretty good laugh at George Orwell right about now. And while it would be nice if L. Ron Hubbard were still alive, the TVs are big, the explosions are loud and colorful and the acronyms are catchy. We have Dolby stereo most of the time, and the reception is usually pretty darn good. And then there's the Internet. All this—and no aliens! Our modern world makes our modern lives A-OK. Of course, there is the "cyber" problem. But they'll probably come up with a computer to fix that. Technology is good.

Pointing your browser

Risqué jokes involving "joysticks" and "hard drives"

Using the phrase "digital convergence" in conversation without laughing

Having carpal tunnel syndrome

"Cross-platform development"

"Killer App"

Bragging about the amount of RAM on your desktop

Bragging about the size of your Internet connection

Screen savers

Personalized screen savers

Pornographic screen savers (Bonus: masturbating to a personalized pornographic screen saver)

Talking about computers after work

Talking about computers at dinner

Talking about computers at a party

Talking about computers when asked for the time

Talking about computers during sex

Talking about computers while sleeping

Talking about computers while masturbating

Using the word "yesteryear"

Meeting people in "chat rooms"

Using a powerbook in a café

Cyber-themed cafés

Using computers in cyber-themed cafés

Using computers in cyber-themed cafés to talk to people in other cyber-themed cafés

Using computers in cyber-themed cafés to talk to people in other cyber-themed cafés about cyber-things (Bonus: while masturbating)

Smileys :)

Peppering e-mail/chat with cutesy acronyms such as "LOL" for "laughing out loud"

Finding Michael Stipe in an AOL chat room

Finding Courtney Love in an AOL chat room

Finding Courtney Love on MTV

Finding Courtney Love in *Rolling Stone*

Finding Courtney Love in *Spin*

Finding Courtney Love in mud-wrestling match with Sofia Coppola for title of "Most Incomprehensibly Ubiquitous Celebrity" (Bonus: referee is Donovan Leitch)

One computer, two screens

Going to MacWorld

Keeping nonfunctional, out-of-date computer components on your desk because they look cool

Naming discs funny things

Naming discs sexual things

Naming hard drives and printers funny things that go together (e.g., the hard drive is Melanie and the printer is Antonio)

Resting a lit cigarette on a coin-op arcade game while you play

Getting five video game tokens for a dollar

Blowing your allowance on arcade games

Using a straw/Tying a string around a quarter/Using Canadian coins to get extra credits on an arcade game

Atari T-shirts

Using the word "Nintendo" for any game system

Playing video games with your mouth wide open

Talking about how Tetris was a Soviet conspiracy to overthrow the American educational system

Either loving or hating Doom or Myst

Playing Doom against someone else on your network (Bonus: using speakerphone)

Games with a "Boss is coming!" hide feature

Arguing that art on the computer just isn't the same (Bonus: saying "There just isn't any texture.")

Arguing that computers will never replace books

Arguing that computers will never replace books even though you never read books

354. Anything that ends with "-fest"

355. Smelling your own farts

356. Observing Flag Day

357. Being named Flagg

358. When spelling it, saying "… that's with double G's"

359. Body paint

360. Road flare fun

361. Back shaving

362. Popping zits

363. Popping zits on your girl/boyfriend

364. Popping zits on strangers

365. Trying to memorize all area codes

366. Having friends test you on area codes

367. Brillo pad fun

368. Parental warnings

369. Turbans

370. Curlicues

371. Root beer floats

372. Parade floats

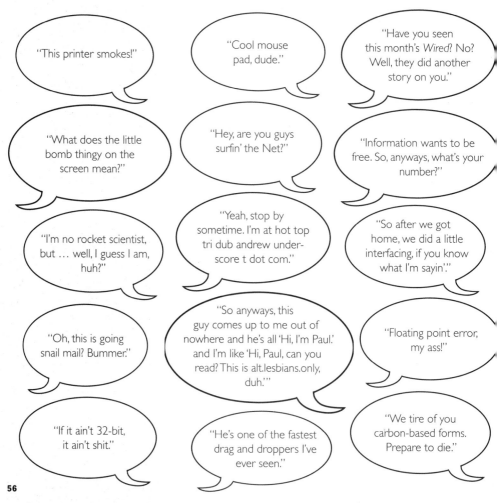

Not owning a TV

Owning several TVs

Saying how you're gonna blow up your TV

Being opposed to fighting games

Games where enemies scream and bleed when they're killed

Confusing SGI with CGI

Confusing SGI with SDI

Confusing SGI with your mother's poppyseed cake recipe

Arguing, "Yeah, but you'll need a T1 to use it."

Confusing T1 with T2

Apologizing for having a cell phone

Explaining that you need it for your job

Getting angry with people who use their cell phone in restaurants

Getting angry with people who are generally happier than you

Excessive use of the F1 key

Eco-friendly computer monitors

"Building on-line communities"

Bitching about the gap between the rich and the poor

Bitching about the gap between the old and the young

Bitching about the gap between the educated elite and the masses

Knowing what COBOL is

People who say ROM when they mean RAM

ISDN

CISC

HTTP

CRT

MIME

ELO

AFL-CIO

SCUBA

RADAR

SOFIA COPPOLA

COMPUTER MONITOR DECORATION CHEESE

A sticker that says "Radioactive" or "Danger: Hazardous Material"

A "This Side Up" sticker, on upside down

Punk band stickers, because even though you use a computer, you're not some geek

Stickers from different countries (on your laptop)

A Buddha statuette

Pictures of Mom

373. Floating decimal points

374. Snap buttons

375. Giving people the right of way

376. Thinking about Aldo Nova from time to time

377. Nicknames (e.g., Chugger = someone who can really put away; Spunky = someone who is y'know, real spunky; Buddha = the fat Chinese guy)

378. Relaxing in the lotus position

379. Pantaloons

380. Pompadours

381. Troubadours

382. Watching Sesame Street as an adult, purportedly to learn from its simple yet profound truths

383. Throwing cashews at the peanut gallery

384. Teasing a seeing-eye dog

political cheese

C'mon, baby, you know it's true: politics is as cheesy as rock 'n' roll is loud and smoking is bad for your unborn fetus. And we love it. We love it so much we hired a guy with a French name to design and build a whole city as testament to just how much we love it. And then we convinced half a million people to live there even though it's like 108 degrees Celsius with 400 percent humidity 22 months out of the year! From the Capitol Rotunda to the cobblestone streets of Georgetown, from the White House ellipse to the Jefferson Memorial and all the way across the Reflecting Pool, Our Nation's Capital is a veritable monument unto itself: Cheese blooms in Washington like psychosis spreads through the feeble mind of Al D'Amato.

Being a wonk

Calling yourself a technocrat

The Louisiana Purchase (suckers)

Having a quorum

Buttering up your alderman

Gary Hart

The Whiskey Rebellion

Carpetbagging

Scalawagging

Gerrymandering

Pandering

Theocracies

Being a liaison

Being an attaché

Being an attaché and pretending

that you're not a spy

Calling spies "spooks"

E pluribus unum

Being a lame duck

Chilling at Camp David the whole time you're a lame duck president

Ramming your bill through Ways and Means

The Kingfish, Huey Long

Speaking softly and carrying a big stick, tee hee

Ranking members of the Senate

Calling the State Department "Foggy Bottom"

Working at Foggy Bottom and playing Risk while on vacation

"just to keep your chops up"

Taking Utrusk from some sissy attaché with only three armies

Bicameral legislatures

Bilateralism

Bipartisanship

Bicycling to the Treasury Department

The fact that the Treasury Department controls all those bad-ass agencies like the Secret Service, Drug Enforcement Agency and the Bureau of Alcohol, Tobacco and Firearms

Xenophobia

The Compromise of 1850

Remembering the Alamo

Referring to the Alamo when trying to get some immigration bill passed into law

Cloturing a filibuster

Singing while filibustering

Reciting poetry while filibustering

Logrolling

Using manifest destiny to explain Grenada and Panama

Explaining what an overwhelming success Grenada was

Imperialism

Those lame-os in Germany who let Christo do his little gift wrapping thing to the Bundestag

The European Economic Community, ha ha

Coups d'état

Draconian measures

Blowing off the Geneva Conventions with the rationalization "all's fair in love and war"

Tories

Bribing an ombudsman

YOU GOT CHOCOLATE IN MY PEANUT BUTTER LIST #3

INTERNATIONAL DIPLOMACY CHEESE/ TOASTER CHEESE

When you're at the U.N. or something and everyone has those little namecards that have your name above the name of "your country"

Having a little flag of "your country" on your desk, too

"Diplomats" from "countries" like "Suriname"

Interpreters with headphones

Waffles

Watching the little wires get red

Watching something toast, and guessing when it'll pop up

Watching something toast, and guessing when it'll pop up using a countdown

Pretending the little knob works ("Today I want my toast just a little darker than usual ... I'll just adjust this toast darkness selector aaaaand ... yep, that'll do the trick!")

Toasters built for extra-wide bread

Buttering the toast *before*

Looking at yourself in the toaster reflection

Kissinger

---

385. Going out with Canadians

386. Acting like you care about them and wouldn't dump them the minute a half-decent American walked by

387. Naming your dog "Dogma"

388. Double dating

389. Double dipping

390. Double daring

391. Derring-do

392. Dippity-do

393. Milk carton regattas

394. Log cabins

395. Using log cabins for a romantic getaway

396. Using log cabins for you and the boyz to hang low for a while

397. Indoor gardening

398. Whittling

399. Believing in sub-atomic particles

400. Using the old finger-in-the-coat-pocket "I've got a gun" trick

401. Butterfly kisses

402. Geometric designs

CAMPAIGN CHEESE

Kissing babies

Pressing the flesh

Soft money

Stars on everything

Big smiles

Position papers

Being introduced everywhere as "The next …"

Campaign theme songs

Campaign theme songs by Fleetwood Mac

"Four more years! Four more years!"

Ordering pizza

Posterboard

Making mean commercials about the other candidates

Making mean commercials where you refer to some obscure statement the opponent said ten years ago, which in fact *was a lie!*

Ending it with, "C'mon, Bill, no more lies."

"Vive le roi!"

Being "plus royaliste que le roi"

Saying, "He couldn't be elected dogcatcher!"

Talking about yourself in the third person

Pounding the podium for effect, but not too hard or they'll think you're crazy or too angry to lead

"I need to know how much a gallon of milk and a dozen eggs cost, and I need to know now!"

"I will not lower myself to the negative campaigning of my fuckhead opponent."

"Next question."

ULTRANATIONALIST DEMAGOGUE CHEESE	**VS.**	THINGS TO DO WHEN YOU DON'T GET ENOUGH CHICKLETS FOR YOUR QUARTER CHEESE
Think that you should take back land legimately sold to/won by other countries	⟷	Say "What a gyp!"
Try frantically to tie religion to politics, and promise voters that you will enforce, from your desk in Washington, the brand of morality that you find appropriate	⟷	Shake the machine and say "C'mon!"
Spend money, run for office and lose	⟷	Kick the machine
Get the ultranationalist babes	⟷	Say "That's bogus!"
Blame foreign people for the country's problems	⟷	Ask your mom for another quarter

HOLDING OFFICE CHEESE

Shredding

Holding things up in committee

The Rotunda

Free stuff from lobbyists

Slush funds

Air Force One

The Vice President's Official Residence at the U.S. Naval Observatory

Dan Quayle's putting green there

The Beltway

First Pets

Getting the seal of your office on all kinds of shit, like coffee mugs and golf balls and stuff

Having a flag in your office

Covert shit, like wars

Disinformation

Junkets

Press conferences, like you really care if people know what's going on or not

Calling reporters by their first name, like "Helen" and "Brit"

Football metaphors ("We'll do an end run around all the god-damn TV people" or "We've got a first and ten and another four years on the game clock!")

Leaks

Giving a leak, then reading about what "informed sources say" in the next day's *New York Times*, and chuckling softly to yourself

Writing your memoirs and dissing all your former staff

PLANE CRASH CHEESE

Putting the child's oxygen mask on first

Holding hands with the total stranger next to you as you go down

Praying, even though you aren't really religious

Sliding down that rubber raft slide thing

Using your seat cushion as a flotation device

Bonding with other crash survivors

Telling your companions you love them as you plummet to your death

Screaming "My baby!" as you're rescued from the burning wreckage

Making a deal with God to spare your life

The flight attendant landing the plane

403. When you're playing basketball with girls and you tell them that they're skins

404. Mint jelly

405. Mint jelly served alongside a pork product

406. Referring to your significant other as "The Old Man/Old Lady," "The Squaw" or "The Boss"

407. Motioning for the audience to stop applauding

408. Helping your fellow man

409. Hitting every button on the elevator as you leave

410. Somersaults

411. Balconies

412. Falconry

413. Masonry

414. Masons

415. Bow ties

416. Bow shaped pasta

installment 4
ENTERTAINMENT

screen cheese, big & small

Bacon, lettuce and tomato. Roosevelt, Churchill and Stalin. The Father, The Son and The Holy Ghost. Television, movies and cheese. The Big Three indeed. Is there some old saying that perfectly introduces, explains and sums up the overwhelmingly obvious and unfathomably pervasive character of life in 2-D? Some bit of witty erudition that effectively captures the one telling truth within the unwieldy conventions, concepts, effects, nuances, panderings and hidden strengths of "the silver screen" and "the boob tube?" Something that combines the moronic, but celebratory, "Hooray for Hollywood!" with something Gore Vidal might say, like "television is the most sincere form of imitation"? Something with the depth of Meryl Streep, the sincerity of Jimmy Stewart, the roguish good looks of Sean Connery, and the irrepressible brand of kookiness and fun favored by that guy from "America's Funniest Home Videos?" Is there any combination of words that can match the emotions of the theme songs from *Chariots of Fire* and "Family Ties?" Is there some sort of phrase that's full of bad and good and love and hate and action and romantic comedy—one that wraps up with a warm and happy ending? No

MOVIE CHEESE

Movies where two enemies unite to defeat a common foe and find out that they're not so different after all

Covering your face with your arm when your car goes over a cliff

Checking under lamps for listening devices

Happy endings

Sad endings

Bittersweet endings

Endings that make you rethink what this whole movie was all about (Bonus: it was all a dream!)

Calling L.A. "Tinsel Town"

Knowing the difference between a best boy and a gaffer (Bonus: knowing what a foley artist is)

Movies that start with a story told in big, bold-faced type scrolling over the screen

Movies that start with a location and a date in little type in the bottom of the screen (Bonus: The movie's set in the future and the type looks *futuristic!*)

Rain machines

Wind machines

Dry ice

Having your best friend race in your place when you're injured

Getting thrown through a window

Getting "shown the door"

Being kicked out of the back door of a club into some garbage cans

Knocking someone out and then dressing up in their clothes (Bonus: Oops—the clothes are too small! Hope no one notices!)

Morals

Morality

Plot twists

Shooting a guy on a second floor balcony so that he breaks through the banister and falls to the ground (Bonus: he lands in a swimming pool or, better yet, a watering trough!)

Knowing that even though this guy is playing hard to get, he's humble and sensitive and will fall in love with the beautiful but shy and adorably insecure female character forever eventually

Waiting for him to recognize her inner beauty

The Vaseline-smeared lens close-up

417. Ordering "healthy" food at a fast food restaurant

418. Plant food

419. Bordeaux

420. Dauphin

421. Dolphins

422. Fins on cars

423. Saying "fin" at the end of a movie

424. Applauding at the end of a movie, like the actors can hear it

425. Target practice

426. Believing that the Ten Commandments are meant to be observed only metaphorically

427. Getting whipped with licorice

428. Ham radio

429. White people

430. Immediately discussing the movie the minute you're out of the theater

Overuse of clowns

Death as represented by the Grim Reaper

Muscular boys

Existentialism

Depravity

Old people thinking back on more innocent times

Pasta

Fountains

Strawberries

Fluidity of time

Surf

Self-doubt

Peasants

Manipulating shadows

Alienation

Romanticism

"Symbolism"

Virgins

Cigarettes

Bicycle thieves

Taking a trip that winds up being a trip back into your past

Well-dressed people

Thinking about God

Too many subtitles

The drug dealer/murderer who redeems all the bad he's done with an act of tenderness and unbelievable self-sacrifice at the end of the movie

After seeing *Say Anything*, deciding that what you need in your next boyfriend is a sense of humor

Movies about making movies!

Old black women that know about the spirits

Adults with special understanding of children's stuff

Movies where a father and son inexplicably swap bodies and have all sorts of crazy identity-confused adventures

Saying goodbye in the rain

Running after a train while waving

Falling in love with a mysterious female with radiant skin and a penchant for nudity only to discover that she's actually an alien or mermaid

When a cop stops a getaway car by shooting its tire

Bad guys who can't control their car when it gets a flat tire

When the killer's looking for someone in a house, and he sees a pair of shoes sticking out from under the drapes. Doesn't he know that's just a clever ruse?

Lawyers who are running late so they put on their suit jackets while running into the courtroom (Bonus: they *still* win The Big Case!)

Undercover cops who wear their badges on their belts

Desk sergeants who yell, "And goddamn it, no press!"

Movies that run the outtakes during the credits

Going behind the scenes

Man, feeling very reckless and lustful, knocks everything off dresser, and they do it right there and then! (Bonus: The woman gets crazy turned on!)

Casting a beautiful actor and a beautiful actress in the same movie, so there's something for everyone

Sidekicks who get a makeover from the main character

Sidekicks who become beautiful and popular after the makeover

Extras rehearsing on the set

Screenwriters hanging out on the set

Stars showing up *all* fucked up (Bonus: *and* late!)

Extras showing up all fucked up

Wrap parties

Fistfighting in the cab of a moving truck

Knowing that whoever gets thrown out the door or through the windshield first is somehow going to be the one who ends up driving the truck

The "lousy basketball team-getting their act together" montage of balls going into baskets set to music

Sleeping your way to the top

Sleeping your way halfway to the top

That little lens-like thing around your neck that lets everyone know just exactly who the director is here

Closing the set for nude scenes

Helicopters

Helicopter attachments (i.e. pontoons, safety harnesses, gigantic magnets)

The helicopter/automobile chase scene (Bonus: the helicopter/car chase scene that ends with the helicopter blocking the car's path) (Double Bonus: the helicopter/car chase scene that ends with the helicopter crashing into a mountain or tunnel!)

Serenades

The two black circles "through the binoculars" shot

The single circle "through the periscope" shot

The single circle with cross hairs "Through-the-sniper's-rifle" shot

Sucking face in the foamy surf

Pregnancy scares

Male pregnancy scares

Having your suspension postponed and your badge reinstated so you can catch some crazy, psycho mastermind archvillain because you're the best, dammit

Cutting French directors slack when you're talking about sexism in movies because, you know, they're *French*

Christ imagery

Using frosted glass to convey the beauty and sensuality of the female body

Movies from Canada (Bonus: dubbed into English)

Ghosts who get all wistful as their still-living lover flirts with a delivery person

Viewing the driver's eyes through a car's rearview mirror

Directors who wear berets

Directors who wear baseball caps (Bonus: with the logo of the movie they're shooting on it)

431. Playing good cop/bad cop

432. Truck stops

433. Harem pants

434. Chain letters

435. Chain gangs

436. Believing that there's some common ground between Eastern and Western philosophy

437. Tazers

438. Numerology

439. Spurs

440. Sword swallowing

441. Robert Schuller

442. Loving music

443. Loving nature

444. Loving just being alive, you know?

445. Goggles

446. Using tomato juice to get the skunk smell out of the dog (Bonus: thinking it'll work)

447. Pocket watches

448. Believing in God

449. Forked tongues

big guys with big hearts on the big screen

THINGS THAT BIG, STRONG, TOUGH GUYS HAVE A SOFT SPOT FOR	THINGS THAT BIG, STRONG, TOUGH GUYS FIND ABSOLUTELY IRRESISTABLE	THINGS/PEOPLE FOR WHICH THAT BIG, STRONG, TOUGH GUY CUTS NO SLACK
A dead wife or lover	A dead wife or lover if the big strong tough guy had something to do with why she died	The bad guy who, needless to say, also had something to do with the death of the former wife/lover
A youngster that follows him around even though he tells him to "Beat it, kid"	A youngster that helps him get over the dead wife or lover and finally open up again	The parents who kicked the youngster out of the house
Beautiful women in vulnerable positions	Tough female cops with big guns	Guys who wear women's clothes
Sex in her bathroom, with bubbles	Sex after a massive fight with the bad guys, with his blood and dirt somehow escaping her nice white silk blouse	The first thirty seconds of a sexual encounter (he always starts out so rough!)
The plight of minorities in American culture	His partner (who is black)	Voodoo
Good luck charms, like a favorite belt or necklace that he always wears	Good luck charms that have a connection with his past, that he almost loses during the underwater fight scene—he dives for the charm when he hardly has time to save himself!	Snakes
Dogs	Dogs that get him beer from the fridge	Whining, unless it's from a dog that's cold or hungry

Directors who sit in folding chairs with their names stenciled on the back

The ol' "I-was-so-drunk-last-night-so-did-you-and-I-do-anything-and-by-the-way-who-undressed-me?" line

Opening a switchblade to make a point

Cocking a gun to prove your willingness to use it

Pumping a shotgun to prove your willingness to use it (Bonus: one handed!)

The we're-so-in-love frolic around Manhattan, featuring ice cream cones, carriage rides through the park and a Brooklyn Bridge kissing shot

Driving a car through a fruit stand

Driving a car through a flower market

Driving a car under a truck, shaving off the roof (Bonus: the pursuing villains/cops forget to duck—guess we won't be getting any more trouble from *them*!)

Going to a penthouse to meet the sexy-but-evil temptress (Bonus: she offers you a drink!)

Parking the surveillance van up the street

Getting discovered in the surveillance van parked up the street

The "panning up from the high heels of the sexy but evil temptress" shot

Best friends finding out at the end of the movie that they are ideal lovers

Calling movies "pictures"

Call a movie a "great show"

Calling a movie a "sleeper hit"

Calling a movie a "chick flick"

Saying a gang film is "so realistic"

Relating to the mysticism in Latin films

Saying someone "knows too much"

Evil villains in wheelchairs (Bonus: petting a cat with gloved hands)

The fact that when you kill a drug dealer you inherit his funky apartment and very often his girlfriend (Bonus: she rides a motorcycle or high-performance automobile)

Wanting to learn to dance like in *Dirty Dancing* (Bonus: figuring out exactly what that dance is)

That last bit of racy dialogue before a hot dance scene

450. Most mesh

451. Stringing anything up a flagpole

452. Putting a lampshade on your head at a party

453. Reaching for the stars

454. Reaching for the star despite their bodyguard throwing you to the floor and putting a knee in your back

455. Elves

456. Elves who make wooden toys

457. Elves who make wooden toys but really want to be dentists

458. Sliding down a banister

459. Sliding down a banister and hitting your nuts on the newell post

460. Pork pies

461. Pork pie hats

462. Turning the other cheek

463. Flinching

le science de la cinéma

SITUATION	LA TWISTÉ	AVEC VERVE!
Car chase	Car goes the wrong way down a one-way street	Car goes the wrong way down *train tracks!*
Villain dies	Villain doesn't really die, but gets up one last time only to have his revenge quelled by a *woman*	Villain's brother (who has an uncanny resemblance to the original villain, even for a family member) arrives to avenge his brother's death ... *in a sequel!*
Woman takes a swing at man	Man stops pathetic attempt to hit him by catching her wrist	Man pulls woman to him by the wrist for a passionate kiss with tongue!
Roadtrip!	Roadtrip in a convertible!	Roadtrip in convertible with passengers' legs hanging outside of car when not picking up cute hitchhikers!
Man goes to prison	Man in prison cares about flower or bird	Prison guard destroys flower or bird to break man's spirit!
Guy has crush on girl	Guy goes to spy on girl, who lives in a sorority	Sorority girls participate in group shower or pillow fight!
Cop and dog team up	Dog runs in front of a bullet, saving cop's life	Dog's girlfriend gives birth to a whole bunch of dogs that look just like dog!

SITUATION	LA TWISTÉ	AVEC VERVE!
A makeover	Makeoveree tries on clothes in a montage set to retro music while companion shakes head in disapproval until makeoveree comes out wearing something really snazzy, at which point companion nods and gives the thumbs up	Then they score some guys/babes!
The band's first gig	Band leader is really nervous because the crowd is a bunch of unruly bikers/unruly punk rockers. But the crowd is won over in, like, ten seconds, and starts dancing and clapping	The big record exec comes backstage after the show *with a check* and a totally huge *record deal!*
A chase on foot	A chase on skis	The skiers have guns!
Kids' parents are divorced	Estranged father watches son's Little League game through the fence	Dad was in prison!
Girl dumps guy	Guy tries to win girl back by doing something goofy, usually involving music, and giving girl puppy dog eyes	Girl takes him back!
Hero delivers pithy phrase	Hero repeats trademark phrase or word (as in "You'll see . . . you'll see" or "Fast . . . real fast")	Phrase is repeated, right before he kills the villain!

the true grit of being a private investigator on TV cheese

Packing heat

Carrying an ID badge that says "Private Eye"

Driving a really cool car (Bonus: it's a convertible!)

Having a really cool pad

Having a really cool pad that's actually a boat (Bonus: it's really messy, and you tell all the visitors that your maid has the week off, ha ha)

Dusting for prints with one of those little camel hair brushes

Always finding just the evidence you're looking for when digging through somebody's trash

Tucking a piece in the front of your pants

Tucking your piece in the back of your pants

Shoulder holsters

Crashing some evil rich guy's mansion during his Gala Ball wearing a white tuxedo

Having a sidekick who flies a helicopter

Having a friend who owns a nightclub

Having a sidekick who's black

Pistol-whipping the henchman's lackeys

Quitting/getting kicked off the force because everyone was on the mob payroll except you (Bonus: you hated all the paperwork anyway)

Jumping fences

Calling in a license plate number on the cell phone to your hot babe assistant/researcher chick back at the office

Wearing a sport coat regardless of the occasion

Knocking back a few cold ones at your pad in just a button-down shirt and the shoulder holster

'Nam flashbacks

Getting to narrate your own show

Getting the word on the street from hookers who think you're cute

Having to babysit some rich guy's daughter who just wants to party

Knocking 'em out with one punch

Being ready to take a bullet for your sidekick

Loving the ladies

Ditching the ladies by saying, "Sorry babe, I'm on a case."

Being friends with a cop, fed or computer geek who can scam you evidence on the sly

Pissing off the chief of police by showing up at the crime scene (Bonus: every time he sees you he says, "Well, look what the cat dragged in")

Having a client who's a foxy dame

Screwing your foxy-dame client on the clock

TV CHEESE

Sitcom episodes where the star gets to display her other talent (singing, juggling, baton-twirling)

Calling reruns "encore presentations"

The wacky neighbor

The pesky little brother

The know-it-all older sister

An audience oohing during a kiss

Comebacks

Guest stars

Pets

An audience aahing for an animal or child

An audience clapping for a character's entrance

Arguments in bed where one person wants to talk and the other one keeps shutting off the lights and this keeps going on and on—like a game that's really funny

Out of shape characters who can't keep up with a treadmill at the health club

Phones that ring right berfore the kiss

Breaking a bottle and brandishing it as a weapon

Writing in some cute-as-pie, 6-year-old actress when the rest of the cast starts sucking wind

Saying "Don't be afraid"

Following it with "Be *very* afraid"

Huddling up to whisper a secret plan so the audience can't hear it

Interviews with writers featuring out-of-focus typewriters in the background (Bonus: interviews with actors with movie posters in the background!) (Double Bonus: old movie posters featuring pirates or army guys or something!)

Ensemble skit shows (Bonus: the opening of ensemble skit shows that show cast members one by one with their names written in neon script underneath a picture of them having fun around gritty and glamorous New York City!)

News shows with people running around in the background "getting the news"

News shows that start with that rat-tat-tat-tat of a stock ticker or something

News shows that start with the earth spinning and spinning and suddenly you're in the newsroom!

464. Punishing flinchers with the punch, wipe

465. Giving wedgies

466. Asking for wedgies

467. Putting things in alphabetical order

468. Striving to attain your goals

469. Putting mascara on your chin to give you a cleft

470. Fantasizing about lesbians

471. Police tape

472. Using police tape in your dorm room

473. Thinking that if you can make it *there*, you can make it anywhere!

474. Putting faux brick over real brick

475. Looking at the dinner bill, tossing it to your friend and saying "I wouldn't pay that if I were you"

476. Table legs that look like lion paws

477. Crossing your toes

cartoon cheese

A falling potted plant hits a person on sidewalk

Gratuitous use of construction sites, especially the I-beam

Birds outsmart cats, dogs outsmart cats, cats always lose

Ducks with speech impediments

Cartoon characters never having jobs (like, *paying* jobs)

Trying not to wake the sleeping bulldog

Boss smokes a cigar

Feeling smurfy

Villains' ultimate goal: world domination

Overuse of stilts

Overuse of dynamite

Never enough anvils

Immortality

ACTION	REACTION
Gets teeth knocked loose	Teeth fall to sounds of piano keys
Character runs into cactus and/or gets shot	Takes a drink of water, water comes out of holes
Gets flattened by steam roller	Body expands to sound of accordion
Hand gets smashed by large mallet	Hand gets bigger and smaller to the rhythm of a heartbeat
Runs into frying pan face-first	Cymbal crashes and face conforms to shape of frying pan
Character burns butt	Puts butt in water, water converts to steam

Beautiful models wearing glasses and lab coats pretending to be scientists

Husband and wife detective partnerships

Husband and wife detectives jumping off a building hand in hand

Women who get scared when a guy has to drive aggressively to evade followers

Doing aerobics in front of the TV

Humming the "Jeopardy" theme song while waiting for something

Actually being on a game show

Talk show band leaders who are drummers

Talk show band leaders that bow to the host

Bantering with the camera crew

Dysfunctional families

Racially mixed families

"I'll be strong for both of us"

Borrowing your neighbor's baby to pick up chicks at the single moms' support group

Cars that drive into the back of semi trucks

Dating your boss (Bonus: the whole office knows)

Showing bloopers from the show during the credits

Showing credits

Trying to hide the fact that your family is housing an alien

The token gay character who looks great in Rayon

Dad drinks milk from container, gets busted

Performing an operation on the nurse you're having an affair with (Bonus: she's blackmailing you!)

Reading your sibling's diary

When a middle-aged woman is depressed because it's her birthday so her friends take her out to a strip club (Bonus: the stripper's her son!)

Dedicating an episode to someone's memory (Bonus: he was some lighting dork that no one even liked)

Thinking that this year's "Saturday Night Live" will be good, just like the old days

Game show hosts that run in from backstage

Running a counter-intelligence operation right under the nose of bumbling Nazi officers (Bonus: having to make the Nazi officers seem somewhat competent so that they won't be replaced with smarter officers)

Sister rivalries (Bonus: they enter a chili cook-off!)

Local TV news panda stories

Episode titling (e.g., "Touched by an Angel," "Almost Paradise,""Disaster in Shaft Nine")

When invesigator-types are looking for clues to some big important case using some wicked, badass computer and afterward comparing the data that they fed into the computer against the FBI archives in Washington D.C., the computer comes back with a reply that repeatedly flashes "MATCH"

Overuse of beaches in general

Laughing at the "agony of defeat" skier on "Wide World of Sports"

Never knowing how "This Old House" is going to end

478. Crossing your heart (Bonus: hoping to die)

479. Opposite Day

480. Male cheerleaders

481. Husbands and wives reading in bed side by side

482. Snapping your leather belt in a menacing way

483. Draping your jacket over the back of a chair

484. Hanging a leather jacket up on a hanger

485. Believing, much like the American Indians did, that everything—even inanimate objects—has a soul

486. Intentionally driving down the freeway with your turn signal on

487. Reading along with the Book On Tape while you drive cross-country

488. Believing that brushing your teeth is just a waste of time

489. Piggyback rides

cheese at the arts

When we're not at the dogtrack or eating something, we spend our days in idle pursuit of the high-minded, euphoric bliss that can only be brought about by Culture. The simple grace of a perfectly executed pirouette. The basso profundo in the final act of an opera by Paganini. The crash of the tympani in Beethoven's Seventh. The delicate opacity in a painting by Caillebotte, one of the most underrated urban impressionists. This is the Art that brings a shudder to our breast, a chill to our spine and a tear to our eye. Art that lasts throughout the ages, if only because it appeals to an archaic class of WASPs well-off enough to fund it. We grow weary of so-called "contemporary" art; we are rankled by the audacious arrogance of performance art. We don't understand post-Beckett theater, and frankly, we don't care. Because as long as Rodgers and Hammerstein get produced on Broadway, we know that our Culture is the only true Culture, and that, as such, it will make it onto the side of a coffee cup somewhere.

THE CHEESE OF HIGH CULTURE

Conductor gesticulations

Standing up when the conductor enters, like he's the Pope or something

The Renaissance

Painting murals on the ceilings of churches

Spending your days having paintings X-rayed

Digging it when people call you "Benefactor"

Toe shoes

Ballet dancers with giant cups

Pas-de-deux

Ending compositions with a loud crash so the audience knows when to clap

Swan Lake

The Nutcracker

The fact that there were no female orchestra members before, like, 1988

French horns!

Ballet class for four-year-old girls

Wearing your leg warmers to the market after ballet rehearsal

Playing stand-up bass with a bow

Oboes!

Gargoyles

Flying buttresses

AT THE OPERA CHEESE

Saying "It ain't over till the fat lady sings"

Big helmets

Pronouncing Wagner "Vogner"

Overtures

Arias

The appalling frequency with which the word "aria" appears in crossword puzzles

Stage pyrotechnics

Kiri Te Kanawa

The Three Tenors (Bonus: mentioning them and not really knowing who they are)

The Magic Flute

Historical settings (Bonus: ancient Egypt!)

Contraltos

Citing opera in pop music, like "Verdi Cries" by 10,000 Maniacs

490. Guys who get piggyback rides from girls

491. Buzzing the control tower

492. Knowing about wine

493. Imagining what it'd be like if you were a vampire

494. Using one credit card to pay off another

495. Saving for a rainy day

496. Spending money like mad when it clouds up

497. Double-seated bicycles

498. Skipping

499. Galloping

500. Hopping

501. Triple-jumping

502. Eating spaghetti one string at a time

503. Keeping up on national events, like as if they're not just gonna go changing everything on you, like, next week

GREEK TRAGEDY CHEESE/ SHAKESPEARE TRAGEDY CHEESE

Dead kings giving advice

Singing omens

Suicide

Wrongly diagnosing suicide

Blaming the messenger

Serenades

Poison-exuding gowns

Golden corded bows, torches of pine

Marrying too soon after a husband's death

Marrying the new king for his status and pretending you're in love

Not knowing who your parents are

Throwing up your hands and thinking the gods are in control anyway, what can we do?

Saying "It's *my* crown"

Having a chorus repeat the king's words to you, loaded with the opinions of mainstream society

Mixed messages

Martyrdom

Playing the "women are different and shouldn't fight" card

Prophecies coming true in the end, but, because there's so much confusion along the way, everyone dies anyway

Repenting at the end, but, alas, it is too late

AT THE MUSEUM CHEESE

The fact that most museums are modeled on ancient Greek architecture

Knowing the difference between Ionic, Doric and those prissy Corinthian columns

That armor wing at the Art Institute of Chicago, and the fact that you have to walk through that crap to get to any other part of the museum

"The Met" (Bonus: romantic comedies featuring scenes at "The Met")

The humidity/temperature monitors in every single room

Renting the headset for the exhibition

Eating at the Museum Café

Sculpture gardens

Buying the print from the show

Buying the book from the show

Being a Friend of the Museum

Saying it was better in New York

Saying it was better in Paris

Taking notes in a museum

Not liking the crazy new stuff they call "art"

Scoffing

OVERHEARD AT THE GALLERY

"Yeah, I'll buy it. Now, you're sure he's dead, right?"

BROADWAY CHEESE

Buying the tape in the lobby

Buying the T-shirt in the lobby

Saying "It was better in London"

Two-fers

"Theatre people"

Off Broadway

Off Off Broadway

Off Off Off Broadway

Performance spaces in lofts with lots of gay people

Becoming a huge Carol Channing fan

Scalping

Playbills

Reading playbills

Pre-theater dinner

Post-theater dinner

Sneaking something to munch into the performance

"Munching on" anything

Quoting Shakespeare

Quoting Simon

Quoting Bogosian

Usher/actors

Actor/ushers

Waiting by the stage door

Stagehands

Julie Andrews

Looks 10, Dance 3

Finales

Encores

SROs

Lindy's

Sardi's

"Restaurant row"

Engineering one of those little accidents with a sandbag, a rope and some stage lights when one of the other cast members is getting a little too big for her britches

The Marriot Marquis

Understudies

Calling actors "players"

Serious emotional dramas that are made into musicals with dancers and heartfelt renditions of timeless songs!

Musicals that make use of roller skates

Plays with naked people

Curtain calls

Picks

Pans

Notices

Pretending not to read the picks, pans or notices

Madonna

504. Questioning authority because a bumper sticker told you to

505. Serenades

506. Giraffes in love wrapping their necks around each other

507. Banana seats

508. Believing in noblesse oblige

509. The Welsh

510. Sutures

511. Furrowing the ground

512. Raising an eyebrow

513. Licking your lips

514. Licking your lips at an all-you-can-eat buffet

515. Drooling

516. Using a tourniquet for non-emergency purposes

517. Clavicles

518. Doing things "for kicks"

519. Putting lip marks on your correspondence

musical cheese

First, there was silence. There was nothing to be heard. It was all quiet-like. There were no chilling, icy-perfect opening chords of electric guitar, no explosions of rock-your-fillings, churn-your-stomach drumbeats, no sudden earthquakes of deeeep, throobbbbing bass in your face. Back then, you had to live with silence—even before you went out, even while you were getting ready. Remember this silence. Remember it as Richie Sambora and US3 and Van Halen and the Beastie Boys and Pavement and Paula Abdul and The Clash and the soundtrack to *Raiders of the Lost Ark* infuse you with a kinetic current of adrenaline. Remember this as you "get psyched," as you "get pumped." Remember as you stand half-naked in front of the mirror blissfully, gloriously exalted, powerful, magnetic… as you prepare yourself to become one with the night. Remember! Scream! Dance! Change your outfit! Change your outfit again! Remember again! Then go see a thousand faces—AND ROCK THEM ALL.

BEING IN A ROCK BAND CHEESE

Closing your eyes while you sing

The "No chicks at practice" rule

The lit-cigarette-in-the-guitar-strings deal

The facing-your-amp guitar solo

Bass solos

Wammy bars

Slap bass

Dropping or breaking a stick and still playing without skipping a beat (literally) because YOU FUCKING ROCK!

Pointing to someone in the audience

Playing a really powerful chord and then pointing to someone in the audience before hitting another powerful chord

Harmony

Concert T-shirts that have a list of the shows and dates but have a stamp that says "Sold Out" over *every last show!*

Saying the word "venue" and meaning it

Wearing the shirt from the last tour to this year's show

Bringing members of the opening band onstage for the big finale

The Howard Jones guitar/keyboard thing

Breaking strings

Breaking sticks

Breaking hearts

Misspelling words in band names on purpose

Playing in drag

See-through plastic instruments

Dolby sound (Bonus: calling it "Dubly")

Marshall stacks

European tours

Being big in Japan

Bands from England singing like they're from Georgia

Bands from Berkeley singing like they're from England

Duct tape

The Ball Boy at Wimbledon/Roadie-on-Tour hunchback scamper across stage

Terrycloth wristbands

Playing on a barge or rooftop

Spoken word bridges

Thanking cymbal manufacturers in your liner notes

Taping spare picks to the mike stand

Courteney Cox's "Dancing in the Dark" video cameo

520. Bits o' Honey

521. Sashaying

522. Snow

523. Some types of rain

524. Beeping things

525. Cheese graters

526. Taking it one day at a time

527. Magic

528. Magician's assistants

529. Doing anything till you hurt

530. Muenster

531. Patio furniture

532. Right/left combos

533. Newborn colts that wobble around on their legs like sissies

534. Knocking over the newborn colts—oops, accident!

535. Being a certain "type" of person

536. Liking a certain "type" of person

537. Liking a typist

Flangers

Having a soundman named Cosmo

Drinking bottled water onstage

Toweling off

Returning for the encore with a towel around the neck and no shirt

Band members leaving stage arm in arm

Analog vs. digital arguments

Left-handed drum sets

The Paul Shaffer end-the-song-n-n-n-n-NOW! gesture

Encores in general

Hiding behind your amp

Battles of the Bands

Curse-word stickers on guitars

Eating fruit onstage

Musical "integrity"

Earplugs

Set lists

Being in the audience and writing down the set list

Calling yourself a jazz band because you don't have a singer

Doing tricks with the mike

The guitarist/bassist back-to-back guitar solo

Songs about being on the road

Naming your band after a disease

Playing by ear

"Label interest"

Twins in the same band

Jumpsuits/kilts

Clap machine/clap sample

Between-song banter

Explaining every song before you play it

Bringing your girlfriend on tour

Bringing your children on tour

Bringing your children onstage

Farewell tours

"We Love You Good Night!"

Asking the crowd if they are ready to rock and roll tonight

Asking it again when you know damn well they heard you and responded the last time (Bonus: saying you couldn't hear it from "the people in back")

Surfing the audience

Surfing the audience against your will

Saying "Hello, Houston!"

Saying "Thank you, Detroit!" (Bonus: getting the city wrong, both times)

Getting out of a limo, drunk, shirt unbuttoned, sunglasses half on, model on your shoulder, smile on your lips, cigarette in your mouth (barely) and chortling, "Where are we? Where's the gig? Oh shit, look at all these *people*!"

HIP HOP CHEESE

Opening your song with gunshots

Pseudo-improv studio conversation

Pseudo-intellectual rap critics (Bonus: they're white!)

"Everybody say, 'Ho-oh!'"

Flow (Bonus: flava!)

Stunts and blunts

Timbos (Bonus: kangols!)

Having NBA guys on your album (Bonus: in your video!)

Frontin' (Bonus: representin')

Pagers

Triplefat Goose

"Hellz yeah"

Having "the skillz that pay the billz"

Visors to the side

Rhymin' about your dick

Dissing sucka MCs

The 808 (Bonus: the human beatbox!)

Coming straight out da ghetto

Coming straight from da streets

Bringin' that beat back

Breakin' it down

Rockin' on and on, till the breaka dawn

Shout-outs (Bonus: to the five boroughs) (Double Bonus: to Afrika Bombaata!)

The fake white guy voice

Sirens

Suffixes (-Dog, -Love, -Mack)

Using "yo" at the end of a sentence

Old Skool

Rugged beats (Bonus: raw beats)

Hoes that you knows

Hoochies

Party peoples

Bein' in da house

Saying "brothers got to work it out"

Dropping beats

Being all that (Bonus: and then some)

New Jack Swing

Your ride

Your crib

Your bitch (Bonus: bitches!)

Calling your friends your "niggas" (Bonus: you're white and Jewish)

Keepin' it real

JAZZ CHEESE

Toe tapping

Clarinets

Fusion

Muting your horn with a plunger

Scatting

"Take Five"

Founding a religious cult after your favorite dead jazz musician

Raspy voices

Clapping in the middle of an improvisation

Spending a good portion of your day burnishing

People who tell you that what you're listening to is not actually "jazz" (Bonus: they make the quote signs with their fingers)

"Bird"

"Satchmo"

Soprano sax

538. Hitting people with bats

539. Living for today

540. Dumb people

541. Oh, and politicians

542. Funnycars

543. Charity

544. The glockenspiel

545. Beanies

546. Party time!

547. Hammer time!

548. Sum-sum-summer-time!

549. Having a phone voice

550. Theater people

551. Being a total loser

552. Taking a snoozer

553. Lying down for a spell

554. Throwing back beers

555. Kicking back

556. Kicking it

557. Tartar sauce

558. Saying "OK, shoot"

THE ILLUSTRATED COMPENDIUM OF CHEESE-EXPRESSIVE GESTURES (CONTINUED)

THE BACK TO BACK GUITAR SOLO

THE EYES CLOSED, TWO-HANDED
POWER BALLAD MICROPHONE GRIP

THE "KEEPIN' IT REAL"

THE "FOR THOSE ABOUT TO ROCK,
WE SALUTE YOU" SALUTE

That John Coltrane "Blue Train" poster everyone has on their goddamn walls

"Monster" players

Having a son who's a rapper

DJ Jazzy Jeff

Acid Jazz (Bonus: Vol. 1)

French jazz bootlegs

The way people always say the French really appreciate jazz

Playing Dixieland at a funeral

Spit valves

Jazz singers

The Jazz Singer

Having good chops

Having puffy cheeks

Having to wear sunglasses all the time

OVERHEARD AT THE DINNER JAZZ CLUB

"Whoa, I didn't even notice that band over there."

BLUES AND SOUL CHEESE

Harmonica solos

Slide guitar

Songs about drinking

Songs about a woman

Songs about a drinking woman

Songs about a mean drinking woman

Songs about a mean drinking woman with one leg (Bonus: in Memphis)

Beale Street

Jeri Curl

Honkies

The Blues Brothers

Marvin Gaye tributes

Don Cornelius

Soul groups that employ bubble-lettering

Singers that "got da blues so bad" they got to do something about it (Bonus: like write a song!)

Blues songs with "Blues" in their titles

Being sad all the time

Growling when you forget the lyrics

559. SWAT teams

560. Being really annoyed with people PDA-ing (Bonus: saying "Get a hotel!")

561. Prefacing an argument with "I'm here to say that…"

562. Wearing pantyhose on your head when committing a crime, like that really makes a difference

563. Wearing pantyhose on your head when not committing a crime

564. Knowing that Rhoda's apartment was 9E

565. Caring about stuff

566. Ads for drummers

567. Same dif

568. Big whip

569. Big whoop

570. Big whoop-di-doo

571. Jaundice

572. Flowers

573. Candlelight

A Brief History of Cheese

4 billion years ago
First life on Earth

430,000,000 B.C.
Jawless fish

250,000,000 B.C.
Pterodactyls, flowering plants, fungi

249,000,000 B.C.
Everyone starts wondering whether this time-line will adhere to any sense of scale, or be even remotely accurate.

200,000,000 B.C.
The powers that be benevolently grant time-line makers the right to toss out, in a wholesale sort of way, any sense of scale. Accuracy is optional.

65,000,000 B.C.
South America cut from Africa, postponing, for millions of years, the development of the bossa nova and the samba.

Sometime here B.C.
God makes Eve out of the rib of Adam, gets Nobel for genetic engineering.

3,700,000 B.C.
Knucklewalkers become passé when certain "progressive" apes look into bipedal locomotion.

3,000,000 B.C.
Savannah-living hominids create first slo-mo scenes of lovers running through tall grass toward each other.

1,500,000 B.C.
Homo erecti— early prototypes for high school football players (dim-witted, stocky, and with large neck muscles)—scavenge with cleavers.

300,000 B.C.
Pan invents his flute. Zamfir makes note.

MISC. HISTORICAL CHEESE: Robespierre • Waterloo • Saying someone else's big defeat was their Waterloo when they're not

100,000 B.C.
Thick-browed, cave-bear-worshipping Neanderthals live in Neander Valley in Rhine Province of Germany and La Chapelle-aux-Saints in France—already, they are developing an attitude.

30,000 B.C.
Humans enter Australia, discover mammals that lay eggs. And, unfortunately, Jane Campion.

23,000 B.C.
Ceramic Venus figurines and cave paintings of wounded bison are all the rage in the Upper Paleolithic art scene. Wine and cheese combo popularized among the smug.

10,000 B.C.
Agriculture begins; chia pets still a ways off.

3800 B.C.
Mesopotamia, the world's earliest civilization, includes cities like Uruk, Ur, Ubaid and Eridu; they use pictographs to record on clay tablets. Many believe history begins with them and their primitive Etch-a-Sketches. They also use kilns.

3100 B.C.
Cats are domesticated in Egypt. Soon followed by cat toys, cat calendars and people who introduce houseguests to their cats.

1250 B.C.
Monotheistic faith revealed to Moses at Mt. Sinai. Idol-worship, sadly, is out.

c. 500-300 B.C.
The Chinese Eastern Chou dynasty produces Confucius, Taoist meditation, and yin-yang philosophy. Yoga on the way.

ANCIENT ROMAN CHEESE

Aqueducts

Tony Curtis and Kirk Douglas

Trojans

The way they tried to change the HQ of the Roman Empire from Rome to Constantinople and play it off like it was no big deal

The "Caesar" cut—all the rage

Skirts made out of metal

Arches (Bonus: arches that stretched all the way to Gaul!)

Big crazy orgies

Brutus

The Coliseum (Bonus: filling it up with water for staged naval battles)

Throwing people to the lions (Bonus: throwing Christians to the lions!)

Bumper stickers that say "Ancient Greece Sucks!"

c. 75 B.C.
Greeks bring us the first musical theater. Oracle at Delphi is precursor to advice columnists.

218 A.D.
Hannibal's army rides around on elephants.

even Napoleon • Posing for a picture with your hand in your vest and not being Napoleon • Getting exiled to Elba • The

300 A.D.
The main drag of Teotihuacán, a Mesoamerican city with more than 2,000 apartment complexes, is a broad boulevard that connects two large pyramids. First potted ferns in lobbies.

372
Huns enter Europe; the French surrender (more of this to come).

700
Celts: elaborate book decorations, Christianized mythology, and knickers.

866
The people who live in Jorvik, a Viking city where York, England, is now, use bone-bladed ice skates, garter hooks, bone whistles, lyres and panpipes. In addition, they have internal parasites.

MEDIEVAL CHEESE

Flogging the serfs and insisting it's for their own good

Pouring hot boiling oil on the Saxons

Falconing

Chain mail

Chain mail skirts

Horse armour

Spelling armor "armour"

Canonizing someone as a saint despite all their very obvious shortcomings

Swimming the moat

Storming the keep

Sacking the palace

Babbling on and on about the Magna Carta at the archery tournament

William of Orange

Troubadours

Having an egg under your armpit

Kicking the shit out of the Normans for absolutely no reason whatsoever, ha ha ha

Lording over your fiefdom

Jousting with your page, if you know what I mean

Usurping the throne

Tapestries with scenes involving embroidered unicorns

Charlemagne

---

c. 1050
Swahili language created; first use of "Simba" as a nickname for small black children.

1066
Normans invade England, bringing with them feudalism and words like *dancer* and *duvet*. English speakers at the mercy of the French until the late 1900s, when they get back at them by getting "cheeseburger," "yuppified," and "homey" into the French dictionary.

1100
French cultural influences reign in Europe: not just berets, but wine snobs, cigarette holders, body hair, and wispy scarves over little black T-shirts. Cappio commercials spread into Mesoamerica.

1238
The fact that at this point the Kievan state in Russia was overrun by the Mongols is not cheesy at all. There is not much that is cheesy about Russia and its cold, harsh history.

---

way some people mispronounce Appomattox • The Edict of Nantes • The conference at Worms • That intriguing rumor

c. 1270
Sufism. Not only is it a funny-sounding word, but it represents the use of Islamic mysticism in poetry by Persians; Persian literature is revived everywhere from the Balkans to India. Also: turbans!

1300-1500
Italian Renaissance, Hundred Years' War, Hapsburg Empire, Black Death, and Christopher Columbus landing in New World—all overshadow any cheesiness that might be happening at the time.

1513
Juan Ponce de Leon explores Florida coast many years before Jon "Ponch" Ponciarelli explores L.A.'s highways.

1535
Spanish bishop lands on the Galápagos Islands. Cruise ships soon to follow.

1600s
Baroque!

1626
This entry removed by request of the U.S. Air Force.

1692
Salem witchcraft trials guarantee a career, 250 years later, for Arthur Miller and Elizabeth Montgomery

1700s
Rococo!

1733
The flying shuttle and the spinning jenny are used in large cotton factories. The inventions delay, even for just a short while, the development of polyester and rayon.

1793
Louis XVI and Marie Antoinette beheaded.

1820s
Wigs, hoops and ruffles are thrown to the wind.

FRENCH REVOLUTION CHEESE

Storming the Bastille

Croissants

The way those wimps ran around yelling Fraternité! Equalité! Liberté! as if they didn't know they were gonna let the Germans walk all over them in '40

Les Misérables

Peasants (Bonus: peasants with pitchforks!)

That little fake Statue of Liberty in the Seine

Letting them eat cake, then winking and saying, "It's good to be the King."

The little basket in front of the guillotine that catches the dead guy's head

---

about how Iceland was named Iceland to fool the Vikings into thinking it was all icy and snowy, and Greenland was named

1914
First wristwatch. We won't see pocket watches again until the late '90s.

1920s
Jung helps us figure out the female psyche via archetypes and spurs conversations like: "You are, like, so Artemis I can't even believe it." "Like, are you kidding? My competitive edge and boyish style make me so Athena. And don't even try to downplay the extroverted, flirtatious Aphrodite in me—even if I do repress her, it's like maybe because deep down I am more her than anything, you know?"

1878
First commercial telephone

1861
Confederacy splits from U.S. and creates its tacky flag.

1879
First telephone commercial that makes all the ladies cry

1921
Chinese Communist Party founded; members anxiously await Mao-style apparel

1907
Modern dance!

1924
Frozen food invented by Birdseye in the U.S.; grocer's freezers soon follow.

Greenland so they would think it was all great and green • the Big Three (Bonus: DeGaulle tying to pretend he was one of

1930s/40s
Merengue becomes national dance of Dominican Republic, eventually causing the spread of the drum machine far and wide.

1954
Henceforth, cheese explodes upon an unsuspecting American populace with a scope and raw power that is impossible to accurately document here.

1950s
Couples dancing!

1953
Carmen Miranda!

1948
Velcro!

1973
Kissinger

The Big Three) • Banging your shoe on the podium of the U.N. • Remembering the Alamo • Remembering Grenada •

GETTING EDUCATED

school cheese

Back when you were still in school, before you knew Thomas Jefferson was a slave owner, before you knew your teachers smoked, before existentialism sunk in, you were but a malleable slab of clay waiting to be carved into the person you are today. It doesn't matter if you wore Guess, Jordache, Toughskins or Levi's, because under all that grass-stained denim, you were still becoming you. In school, you didn't just learn how to divide 10 into 191 and deal with the one, you learned tetherball strategies, masturbation jokes and how to pop a wheelie. You learned to evaluate people by their clothes and to evaluate clothes by the people that wore them. You learned how to burp. You learned how to lift one cheek to fart. From day one—at age 4—you were sucked into school's yearly cycle, a churning maelstrom where you lost your teeth, tried out friends and haircuts, Oxycuted zits and watched with awe as the mystery of pubic hair unfolded before you. Alas, this tumultuous dance with life was destined to one day end. Before you knew it, the diploma had been signed, the hat had been tossed skyward, and a nearly grown-up you was perched on the starting block of life, armed with opinions, angst and, above all, a smart and distinctly individual but not-too-fussy clothing style.

Being in the rowdy cheering section

Being in the rowdy cheering section without a shirt

At the pep rally, getting your buds together and dressing up like cheerleaders with big huge balloons for boobs, and doing some crazy-funny skit

Decorating lockers with streamers and crepe paper before the big game as a way of getting the players psyched up/whipping the school into a spirit frenzy

Having a pencil sharpener shaped like a race car, frog or football helmet

Having a pencil sharpener shaped like just a plain, old pencil sharpener

Puffy stickers

Smelly stickers

Stickers with googly eyes

Gym teachers who wear those little polyester short shorts made by BIKE

Running down the hall while imitating an airplane because no one else is around

Staying after school on your own accord

Acting out movies like *Grease* (Bonus: you're Sandra Dee)

Getting butterflies when looking at the call-back list for the school play

Hanging with the guidance counselor (Bonus: assuring your friends that you're just in there for the free candy)

Music teachers who were in school during the late '60s and make sure you know it (Bonus: they have you memorize the symbolism in "American Pie" or the "Jeremiah Was a Bullfrog" song)

Playing king/queen of the mountain

Four square

Tea parties in four square

Making a "no tea parties" rule in four square

Being really good at tetherball

Asking "Where's the flood?" when someone's Wranglers are too short

Making a lollipop by wrapping your fruit roll-up tightly around your finger

Relishing the last cheese-saturated Chee-to in a bag of Chee-tos

Rubber cement boogers

Those markers that smell good

Those markers that smell "peculiar"

574. Chivalry

575. Telling the cab driver to "Step on it!"

576. Telling the cab driver to "Follow that cab!"

577. Mustache combs

578. Expansion teams

579. Expansion team fans

580. Patent leather

581. Harris Tweed

582. Shannon Tweed

583. Cutting the proverbial rug

584. Using the word "proverbial"

585. Beer steins

586. Wine glasses

587. Fruit cups

588. Sexual innuendoes about fruit cups

589. Sports cups

590. Plastic silverware

591. Having different boxes for different holiday decorations

592. Leaving them up all year round

PRESIDENT'S PHYSICAL FITNESS TEST CHEESE/KEY CHAIN CHEESE

Having a personalized key chain

Key chains that attach to your belt like you're goddamn Batman or something

Shuttle run

Bottle opener key chains

Sorority or fraternity bottle opener key chains

Key chain with picture of you and your BEST FRIENDS

Arm hang

Key chains that float

Key chain with a device that, when pushed, makes your car make a cool futuristic sound

Standing broad jump

The 440

"Needs improvement"

Strutting down the hall the first day wearing a bra

Wearing lipstick the very next day

Saying "That's so funny I forgot to laugh" (Bonus: imitating laughing while you say it!)

Liking someone

Liking someone short

Keeping your pencils in a box

Pencil wars

Making a gun with your finger and a rubber band

Putting rubbers on bananas in Health class

Getting really into it when reading Shakespeare aloud

Making a birthday present for Mom in shop class

Shop teachers who are missing a digit

Getting your history teacher to buy you beer

Having a particular brand of beer that you buy

Having a cheap beer for the pre-party and a better beer for when the girls arrive

Being the new kid

Beating the new kid

Being the new kid and shakin' the dust off this sleepy town

Getting pictures of your friends in the yearbook because you're on staff

Forging notes to get out of class

Forging notes to get friends out of class

Forging notes for money

Making fake IDs

Making fake IDs from obscure Western states without knowing what that state's real ID is supposed to look like

Pounding brews in the parking lot

Pounding brews in the parking lot, in a pickup

On dress-up day, dressing up as a teacher

On dress-up day, dressing up as a nerd

Blowing off dress-up day because you're too fucking cool

For talent show, getting a bunch of your friends together and doing a dance to a cool song from "Hair"

Finishing with a kickline

Wishing you went to a cool school like the one in "Fame"

Wearing a sweatshirt from the college you want to go to

Getting a permission slip from the folks so you can smoke at school

Riding to school with geeky older siblings and ducking out of sight when they pull into the parking lot

Sharing a locker

Sharing a locker with your sweetie

Carrying your books against your chest

Class rings

Class pets

Class pets named after presidents

Putting cool stickers all over your books because no one ain't going to tell you how to keep your textbooks

Joining a club

Founding a club

Saying clubs are for dorks

Digging the smell of mimeographed paper

Running outside at the beginning of recess

Sauntering back in at the end

Playing sports during recess in your best white cords

Putting laces with red hearts or green frogs in your Adidases

Deciding on a French/Spanish name for French/Spanish class (Bonus: it's *Pierre* or *Gigi!*)

OVERHEARD IN K-12

"Okay, so we're not popular *this* year."

"I'm not talking to you today."

"Him? He doesn't even know how to color!"

"You know about the girls' gym teacher, right?"

593. Being too cool to remember Valentine's Day

594. Celebrating Valentine's Day

595. Calling Valentine's Day "VD"

596. Describing yourself as a "certified chocoholic"

597. Losing your cherry

598. Being preggers

599. Having a bun in the oven

600. Saying the rabbit died, ha ha

601. Eating pickles

602. Being on the rag

603. Girls talking about that time of the month

604. Boys talking about that time of the month

605. Saying "He's afraid of commitment"

606. Saying "She's not ready to settle down"

607. "Settling down"

608. Bisexuality

THE ILLUSTRATED COMPENDIUM OF CHEESE-EXPRESSIVE GESTURES (CONTINUED)

THE "NO, I REALLY, REALLY, *REALLY* HAVE TO GO"

THE "YOU'VE GOT BUNNY EARS AND WON'T EVEN KNOW IT TIL THIS PICTURE COMES BACK" LAFF RIOT

THE "I KNOW THE ANSWER AND MY HAND IS GETTING HEAVY, SO JUST CALL ON ME ALREADY"

THE "PLEASE, PLEASE, PLEASE CAN WE HAVE BIOLOGY OUTSIDE TODAY?"

cticing for a spelling bee

sting to your friends about
y you harassed the substitute
her

unteering to carry books for a
who's on crutches so you can
e class early

shing you were the kid on
tches

ting excused from gym class
ause you have cramps

ting excused every week

cling up for a playground fight

ing all bummed when a
cher intercedes in a playground
t

rting a playground fight just to
to get in a quick one when the
cher intercedes

nking your yearbook quote is
ly quite provocative

nting to slow dance in principle
not wanting to get that close
anyone in particular

atching teachers slow dance
ether

atching teachers do the fox trot
onus: they're really hamming it
)

empting to put on lipstick by
ueezing together your boobs,
t like Molly Ringwald did in *The
akfast Club*

eaking out

---

prep school cheese

Having cool, brilliant and icono-
clastic English teachers who
once starred on "Mork and
Mindy" and who teach everyone
about living life to its fullest
and reading poetry and all that
crap, but who still manages to
get one kid killed

Lacrosse

Believing that you were sent
there because your parents
wanted to get you a good edu-
cation, and not because they
wanted you the hell out of the
house because you were an
annoying, pale-skinned chump

Wearing your father's Harris
tweed

Wearing your first set of pearls

Beating the public school kid's
fist with your face

Georgian architecture

Anglophilia

Being 16, looking 12, and buying ether in a Greenwich Village
head shop

Tea as a social event

Still not getting into an Ivy

---

609. Peeing in a bottle

610. Knowing too much
about astrology

611. Calling a 'copter a
chopper

612. Figuring your score
in women's magazine
quizzes

613. Sandals with socks

614. Doing your own
stunts

615. Spit shines

616. Foot massages

617. Mom and Dad

618. Bionics

619. Cryonics

620. Yorkshire pudding

621. Trade secrets

622. Ancient Chinese
secrets

623. Kick lines

624. Honking in tunnels

625. Cheese puffs

626. Folders

627. Crumplers

628. Done deals

629. Saying "it was love
at first sight"

THE JOYS OF LEARNING TO DRIVE CHEESE

Giving the instructor a taste of the dash just to loosen him up

Saying "Hey Teach, c'mon, we gotta lose that sign on top of the car."

Then saying "Alright! Let's troll for babes!"

Getting the emergency brake and the normal brake mixed up

Showing off for the cutie in the backseat

When driving, repeating "Little Shepherd to Lost Sheep, Little Shepherd to Lost Sheep."

Stopping at every intersection even when you have the right of way

Giving cab drivers the finger

Stopping at every intersection when you have the right of way and waving other cars through

Stopping at every intersection when you have the right of way and waving other cars through and then, as soon as they go, you start to go and then slam on the brakes and honk the horn and throw your hands up in the air

Getting the wipers and the turn signal mixed up

Watching that *Red Asphalt* movie in Driver's Ed class

Watching *Red Asphalt* and laughing out loud hysterically

Giving cops the "hang loose" gesture at stoplights

Occasionally slamming on the brakes "just to make sure they work"

Tapping the horn just to let other drivers know you're there

When riding in the backseat, constantly moaning "Oh my god, I'm going to be sick."

When riding in the backseat, looking out the window at pedestrians like you're trapped in a death trap

Laying a patch

Using the Driver's Ed car as a drug mule

Put your hands at the 10 and 2 o'clock positions

Sorry, Chief—this arm's for the babes!

OK, now pay attention.

Oooh, hold on, this song rocks!

Oh my God, we just hit that old woman!

You want I should pull over?

Running away

Bringing your blanket

Having a note for your teacher pinned to your jacket

Having your mittens attached to your jacket with those little clips

Losing the mittens anyway

Riding to school on a pink plastic skateboard

Riding to school on a bike with a banana seat

Seeing if you can kick the same rock all the way home from school

Watching TV shows after school you know are meant for really little kids

Classes that have labs

Lab partners

Getting yourself a lab partner that's smart or cute

Impressing your lab partner with a Bunsen burner trick

Learning yo-yo tricks

Calling your friend a yo-yo

Yodeling

Being at the transitional stage between being called "Petey" and "Pete"

Getting freaked out by an overdramatized/blatant scare tactic TV movie (Bonus: It's about angel dust … or nuclear war!)

Getting freaked out by an overdramatized/blatant scare tactic Sex Ed movie

Lice checks

Getting called into the hallway after a lice check

Sitting next to the guy that peed in his pants

Being the guy that peed in his pants

Husband and wife teachers who work at the same school

Being a boy student and taking Home Ec as an act of rebelliousness/an attempt to meet babes

That ceramic tile on all the bathroom walls

Feigning illness by holding the thermometer against a light bulb

Being hot and cold at the same time

Assuming with every snowfall that school will be canceled

Indoor recess

Eating glue

630. The "keep it coming" underhand car directing gesture

631. Greasing palms

632. Grease monkeys

633. Monkey suits

634. Mistletoe

635. Feeling your mustache stubble (Bonus: trying to bite it with your teeth)

636. Insisting on the Kleenex with the moisturizer crap in it

637. Looking in your used Kleenex after

638. Smelling your garbage when you know it's really bad

639. Funny little gift books

640. "Have a good one"

641. "You know it"

642. "Hot diggity-dog"

643. "Super!"

644. "Super duper"

645. "Lickity-split"

646. Hat/glove/scarf sets

647. Forgetting what you were going to say

college cheese

College! It can wake you up early in the afternoon after a great Tuesday night out and slap you in the face, make you blow off that anthro lecture to go to Prof Wilson's office hours before your econ discussion, run into your old roommate from the dorms freshman year (the one you roadtripped to Buffalo with that first week of school, what a *weirdo*) and still allow you enough time to catch some sun on the Quad. All those ill-fated spring breaks and "motherly" RAs and Finals from Hell somehow combined to form a warm and nurturing cocoon. Jack Nicholson posters became Dali prints that eventually turned into framed Mondrians that hung next to pinned-up rejection letters from prospective employers. Foam egg crates impossibly changed into cool-as-hell broken couches in cool-as-hell off-campus apartments. Even that old boyfriend from sophomore year, the semester you rushed Kappa Alpha Chi, your brief flings with Socialism and your first disease now seem to float on the widening sea of the "best times of your life." Ahhh, could you ever forget beat poetry, "rocks for jocks," that cute TA from lit class or two Buffalo wings for every one pitcher of cheap-ass watery beer? Never again will so much of your time be filled with so little— or is it the other way around? Does it even matter? Like it or not, you will always be property of some institution's athletic department—size XXL.

Buying a patch of carpet for your room

Buying a black light, lava lamp, Christmas lights or any sort of mood lighting for your room

Thinking your newfound mood lighting will increase your chances of getting some

Listening to your roommate have sex

Clandestine mini-microwaves

Clandestine hot plates or mini-crock pots

Boiling water in your room for any reason

Playing sports in the dorm hallway with all your new friends

Being some sort of dorm "official"

Being a dorm official and busting a resident for boiling water, playing sports in the hallway or possessing an unauthorized kitchen appliance

Skippin' class/Blowing off class/86ing class

Going to class high

After-hours parties

Off-campus parties

Parties that start in the daytime

Telling people to have a great break

Cramming for finals

Pulling all-nighters

Having a cartoon on your door

Having your name on your door (Bonus: It's written on a piece of colored construction paper)

Having an erasable marker message pad on your door so you don't miss any of your friends' unscheduled visits

Posters of cool bands

Posters of James Dean

Posters of beer

Getting the Victoria Secret catalogue just to check out the merchandise, wink wink

Orientation games: If you were a vegetable, who would you be?

Strip poker

Talking about strip poker but never playing it

Identifying yourself via musical interest

Putting up a Klimt, Monet or Escher

"The Kiss"

Those "I pay $20,000 a year for this lousy sweatshirt" sweatshirts

Dressing as a vamp or a kitten for Halloween as an excuse to wear skimpy clothes

648. Driving yourself nuts trying to remember what you were going to say

649. Using the phrase "drive nuts"

650. Reading condensed books

651. Chipped nail polish

652. Polish jokes

653. Joke shops

654. Finding out where someone is from and immediately launching into a fake accent "Oh, you're from Boston? Did you paaahk the caaaah?"

655. Anything made to glow in the dark

656. Saying "period" for emphasis ("I'll give you ten minutes. Period.")

657. Sports events crowds that chant "We Will Rock You"

658. Saying "beep beep" when someone's in your way

659. Saying "Bingo!"

660. Playing Bingo

661. Singing "B-I-N-G-O!"

Dorm formals

Having a favorite night out

Nicknames for bars

Nicknames for campus buildings

Nicknames for the library (Bonus: It's a totally ironic nickname like "The Disco!" Ha ha)

Thinking hard about which wall posters best represent you

The undying conviction that each new semester will bring a slew of new romantic possibilities in your classes

Dropping a class after looking at the syllabus

Dropping a class because it starts too early

Dropping a class because there are no romantic possibilities

Meeting at the Quad

Chillin' at the Quad

Playing Frisbee, football or hackey sack at the Quad

Having sex on the Quad

Those diagonal sidewalks that they have all over the Quad to keep the grass looking nice

Missing your mom

Secret handshakes and code words

Not taking secret handshakes and code words seriously

Roommates that are total slobs

Roommates that are total neat-freaks

Roommates that don't understand you and your unique needs

Only showing school spirit when you're drunk in the campus bar

Believing that you're smarter than everyone else in your class

Shotgunning beers (Bonus: someone assists your shotgunning)

Wild acts of desperation very early in the morning

Art history majors

Pretending to take notes in class

Returning from a year abroad and using phrases from that country (Bonus: forgetting the equivalent English phrases)

Returning from a year abroad with an accent

Returning from a year abroad wearing a beret

Putting your bed on cinder blocks

Changing margins/type sizes/line spacing to make a paper longer

Justifying skipping class because you're already late

Justifying criminal activity because you're a student (Bonus: selling drugs for tuition money)

Wanting to learn how to play the guitar

Sleeping with your professor (Bonus: gets you an A)

Using milk crates for shelves

Shower buckets

Wearing flip-flops into the shower because, dammit, there are a lot of germs in there (Bonus: you still get a fungus)

Being uninhibited

Reading a book at the library

Reading the same sentence in a book at the library over and over because you're thinking about having sex with someone sitting across the room

Falling asleep at the library

Falling asleep at the library and dreaming about having sex with someone sitting across the room

Flags as decoration (Bonus: the Confederate flag!)

T-shirts made to immortalize a particular event (Bonus: It has a drawing of or reference to BEER!)

Being exposed to other people's perspectives

Taking up a new smoking habit

Being concerned about your personal growth

Engaging in extracurricular activities to round yourself out

Thinking about things differently

Not knowing the words to your alma mater but humming it anyway

Knowing the words to your alma mater

Projecting yourself into your interpretation of literature ("I think Hamlet wasn't getting as much as he wanted from the ladies.")

To cap a nice date, playing a little guitar to get her in the mood

Double majors

Double minors

Never actually getting around to declaring a major

Hookin' up

Using the word "party" as a verb

Going to see your team play in a bowl game

Trashing the motel room while at said bowl game (Bonus: you graduated 10 years ago!)

Inviting friends from home up for the crazy Spring Fling/Winter Carnival/Block Party Weekend

Inviting boy/girlfriends from home for the Big Dance

Making your boy/girlfriend from home promise not to tell he/she's still in high school

Studying in coffee shops

Pretending to study in coffee shops

Bringing a really deep book to a coffee shop to rest your latte on

Review sessions

Going to review sessions to make up for all that class you missed

Making friends with someone with good attendance/good note-taking skills to get notes from all the class you missed

Calling the guy that always seems to be in the lounge and at all of the dorm activities the "Dorm Guy"

Roommates who come home drunk and piss themselves

662. Ringo Starr and the All-Star Band

663. Blessing yourself after you sneeze

664. Goulashes

665. Recitals

666. Ordering a Surf 'n Turf meal

667. Purposely making eye contact with someone as you're lip synching

668. Use of the haunting mandolin in rock songs

669. Minivans shaped to seem aerodynamic

670. Making the "finger across the neck to denote a slit throat" sign when someone gets fired

671. Ladles

672. Oven mitts

673. Bunk beds

674. Beds shaped like cars

675. Wallpaper that makes it look like you're on the moon, or in some cool forest

676. Whistling with vibrato

BEING A PROFESSOR CHEESE

Wearing sport coats with suede patches on the elbows

Smoking a pipe

Thinking about pithy things all the time

Having a smoke in your office with a student while talking about pithy things

Reading all the time

Forgetting things easily

Being disheveled

Having a crazy-good-looking wife

Acting like you've forgotten the most kiss-ass student's name just to annoy him

Assigning your entire class to access one particular book in the library

Shocking the freshmen by working the word "fuck" into your lecture a few times

Letting all the students introduce themselves on the first day, like you even care

Getting together with other professors to decide when you are going to collectively bury the students in classwork

Wearing those "Grand Dragon" robes to graduation ceremonies

Getting tenure and then blowing off the rest of your career

Intimidating the pretty students

Just being arrogant in general

Roommates who come home drunk and claim they're going to kill themselves

Roommates who come home drunk and claim they're going to kill you

"First semester" best friends forever

High school prom collages

Stealing a sorority composite

Making a fraternity paddle

Hanging a fraternity paddle on your wall

Brandishing a fraternity paddle

Continually making jokes about your school because they have a bad football team

College newspaper feature stories (Bonus: they're about drinking or love on the Internet!)

Beer suppers

Barley breakfasts

Liquid lunches

Getting really psyched when the new J. Crew catalog comes in the mail

Lofts built with some wicked-strong 4" x 4" posts

Tapestries on your furniture

Tapestries on your ceiling

Tapestries hanging from your loft so you can have a little privacy, if you know what I'm saying

Bumper stickers from your college

Bumper stickers of your college mascot

Bumper stickers of your high school

Bumper stickers of Jerry Garcia

Bars where only seniors hang out

Going to bars where only seniors hang out when you're not even a senior (Bonus: The seniors think you're a dork but let you stay because, hell, you've got spunk!)

Lying while giving a campus tour

The "Term Paper Blues?" ad

Being one of those people that meet freshman at the airport (Bonus: you come back to school early in the fall to do it!)

Telling your parents that your school doesn't use grades

Telling your parents that you graduated

Making a speech at a student protest and comparing it to Berkeley in the '60s

Thinking your frat is not unlike the frat in "Animal House" (Bonus: you liken yourself to Otter or D-Day!)

Recording a lecture on one of those little tape recorders

At the beginning of each semester, resolving to take better notes and keep up with the reading in all your new classes

OVERHEARD ON THE QUAD

Oh, Professor, I agree *completely*. You couldn't *possibly* be more right.

Yeah, I was going to go to Harvard, but Boston is so rainy.

The diachronic exegesis in "Justine" is so atypical of Rousseau, don't you think?

Reading list? Nobody said nothin' about no *reading list!*

677. Whistling with vibrato to rock music

678. Reading postings in elevators

679. Asking someone where they got that great outfit

680. Using sparklers instead of regular fireworks, if regular fireworks are, bummer, illegal in your state

681. Wishing you lived in Tennessee, where they can do all the fireworks they want

682. Buying personal hygiene items at flea markets

683. When exaggerating about the size of something, saying it's as big as some midwestern state, like Kansas

684. Light blue bricks

685. Fog

686. Foam

687. Lather

688. Foamy lather

689. Smelly foamy lather

intellectual cheese

College students? Bah! They are mere squirrels, scrambling for a nut under the tree of knowledge next to real Intellectuals—the trees themselves! Intellectuals are students of *life*. Intellectuals study history, revolutions and poetry; in cafés and museums; with pipes, tea and degrees too numerous and weighty to mention. But take heart, even if your cognitive powers pale beside those of the black turtleneck set, know that, like trashing a long-dead author who could wipe his ass with everything you've ever done, no one can escape cheese.

Taking off your glasses to make a point

Making To Do Lists in iambic pentameter

Free associating about streams of consciousness

Noms de plume

Literature about vampires

Saying ye when you mean you

Building shrines to Balzac

Throwing around the word "avatar" conversationally

Assuming that were you a Hindu, you'd be a Brahmin

Calvinism

Dénouement

Shouting "Out damned spot!" when doing dishes or laundry

Quoting Descartes in Latin ("Cogito, ergo sum")

Not being a commie, but still knowing Cyrillic

Writing checks in Cyrillic just to confuse your bank

Speaking in a different language in front of your children so they don't know that you're talking about them

Having a room in your house called "The Library"

Smoking a pipe (Bonus: in The Library)

Gerunds

Participles

Principles

The Dead Sea Scrolls

The Rosetta Stone

Debating the pronunciation of nihilism ("Not neye-a-liz-um, you serf, it's *neee-a-liz-um!*")

Pointing out that the Latin root of nihilism is the same as that of annihilate (a-neye-il-ate)

Describing something as "Grapes of Wrathian"

Determinism

Losing your bifocals all the time

Writing haiku

Using a quill pen

Writing on parchment

Shouting "Zounds!" when you spill your inkwell

Dissing papal infallibility

Saying "say" in the middle of a sentence when, say, you mean "for instance"

Espousing something

Renouncing something

Renouncing materialism

E-mailing your discussion group a renouncement of materialism

Postulating in general

Arguing semantics

Maintaining that the Marquis de Sade gets a bum rap

Quoting *Thus Spake Zarathustra* at dinner parties

Think pieces

Think tanks

Open letters to Congress in the *New York Times*

Authors who have prices on their heads

The Booker Prize (Bonus: the short list for the Booker Prize)

Foreign authors (Bonus: Octavio Paz)

Famous physicists

Winning the Nobel Prize but not really telling anybody

Rhodes scholars

Being a Rhodes scholar and then when you're elected president or something, only appointing other Rhodes scholars

Peppering your speech with foreign phrases (Bonus: ancient Greek)

Insisting on reading literature only in its original language (Bonus: calling it "its native tongue")

Taking issue with translations

Perusing *Bartlett's Familiar Quotations* for something witty to quote at dinner

Ringing up your old classmates when you see your professor quoted in *The Times*

Having a *soirée* at your *pied-à-terre*

Realizing your lover's argument is invalid under tu quoque

Realizing your argument is invalid under post hoc

Finding the Pre-Raphaelites cliché

Reexamining the Brontës

Filling the Kierkegaardian chasm

Stephen Hawking always borrowing your notes

Reading stands (Bonus: with open dictionary)

Cardigans (Bonus: with a vest)

Ladders for bookshelves (Bonus: on wheels)

Mont Blanc pens

One-act plays

Writing one-act plays

Writing one-acts during lunch

Stroking your beard

Calling someone insufferable

Calling a situation untenable

Bashing TV but watching it anyway

Not understanding the jokes on "Roseanne"

Saying "ergo"

Theses

Symbolism

Metaphor

Killing your lover's ex

690. Stucco

691. Anything made from logs

692. Spelling "buses" "busses"

693. Awnings

694. Treating the elderly with respect

695. Laughing to yourself

696. Naming streets after trees

697. Naming streets after towns in England, instead of thinking of new names

698. Coupons

699. Mopeds with the whole pedal thing going

700. Flippin' through the ol' Rolodex

701. Having a Rolodex full of only friends' phone numbers

702. Having cartoon cows cheerfully advertise steakhouses

703. Christmas tree lights with huge flashing bulbs, because Jesus would have liked it that way

TRAVEL AND LEISURE

being on the road cheese

We are a traveling people. Always have been, always will be. We are the sons of Pilgrims and the daughters of Vikings, us Americans. And like our grandparents, we just *love* to travel. We love it when we're young and get to hop out the back of our parents' station wagons to eat homemade sandwiches at sunny rest stops. We love it when we're older and more adventurous, when the open road beckons to us like a black and white movie full of old cars and faded jeans and crazy locals and those dusty looking 1950s gas pumps. We love experiencing new things, and we especially love roughing it. We love airports and roadside diners and trains that speed through the night. We love having a reason to use our Swiss Army knives. We love caves. To us, travel is more than an escape from ordinary life, more than an opportunity to sample different beers and listen to other people talk in funny accents. Travel is the thing that drives us, propels us, makes us go places. Just like Columbus, who discovered the Panama Canal, travelling is in our blood.

BEING ON AN AIRPLANE CHEESE

Armrest wars

Kicking the back of the chair in front of you

Refusing to wear your seat belt

Asking the old lady in front of you if she speaks jive

Saving your free peanuts for the kids at home

Singing along with the song on your headset

Stealing off the headset so you won't have to pay next time

Burying all sorts of garbage in the seat pocket in front of you (Bonus: it's the kind of garbage that will smell real bad if the lazy-ass cleaning crew doesn't stumble upon it)

Searching in your bag and saying "Where in the hell did my gun ... err, gum go?"

Smuggling

Smuggling fruit

Telling the people you sit next to that it's your first time flying ever

Smiling when they say that everything's going to be OK (Bonus: freaking as the plane moves away from the gate)

Being exhilarated by turbulence

Asking the person next to you, "Business or pleasure?"

Waiting until everyone's asleep and then screaming, "Oh my god, what's that out on the wing! Don't you see it?!?"

Making plane noises to yourself

Bringing your own blanket

That little prayer you say to yourself just before takeoff

Asking the flight attendant if you can see the captain

Insisting to the flight attendant that you must see the captain

Saying to the people in first class: "Hey, one of these days I'll be riding up here"

Hitting the reading light on and off to get a funny strobe effect

Leaving a long one in the restroom

People who wear leis going to or from Hawaii

People who wear sombreros going to or from Mexico

Acting as if the G-forces pin you to your seat as the plane takes off (Bonus: rolling your eyes to the back of your head)

Using the telephone to call someone else on the plane

Leaving porn in the back of the seat in front of you

704. Nativity scenes

705. Driving with your knees

706. The Popemobile

707. Saving magazines for their historical value and usefulness as research tools

708. "Bathroom books"

709. Books with lists in them

710. Books about trends

711. Books that try to be funny

712. Books about trends with lists in them that try to be funny

713. Dishwashers

714. Microcassettes

715. When painting something, sticking your thumb out and squinting

716. Shutters

717. Mugs

718. Having a favorite mug

719. Tumblers

720. Tumbling

LAS VEGAS CHEESE/ ANCIENT EGYPT CHEESE

Cat worship	Passing over someone's house just because there's a big bloody X on the door
Papyrus	
Unibrows	
Raising pyramids	
Neglecting to invent the wheel	Swarms of locusts
	Boils
The Fertile Crescent	Polyester leisure suits
Huge earrings and lots of gold chains	17-year-old Pharaohs
	Harems
Men wearing way too much eyeliner	Mummies
	Wearing the same sandals every stinking day
Cleopatra's blunt cut	
Blowing your savings on blackjack	Togas cinched at waist with a gold belt
Profile portraits	Seeing a mirage
Hiding your baby in reeds then floating him downstream	Staying at the Mirage
	Always being compared to Rome
All-you-can-eat buffet for $7.95	

Going to the back of the plane to lie out over the whole row

Checking out everyone at the gate before you take off to see if there are any cuties

Praying/crossing your fingers one of them sits next to you (Bonus: they do!) (Double Bonus: they're great!) (Triple Bonus: you make it with them!) (Quadruple Bonus: it's great!) (Quintuple Bonus: the plane crashes and while they die—you live!)

Wondering if it's a coincidence that the airline flies to all those cool places featured in the in-flight magazine

Putting your seat in its full upright position

Bags in the overhead compartment that shift during flight

Stewardess call buttons

Hitting a stewardess call button by mistake and then pretending you never did it when she comes over

Shaving in the bathroom

Masturbating in the bathroom

Doin' it in the bathroom

"The mile-high club"

Putting on your oxygen mask and then helping your child with theirs

BACKPACKING EUROPE CHEESE

Sporting a bandanna

Drinking beer at the local McDonald's

Hanging out in the hostel bar

Cruising topless beaches

Sleeping on topless beaches

Playing the "name game"

"Small world" comments

Collecting patches from all the places you've been

Canadian maple leaf paraphernalia

Wearing a Canadian maple leaf patch to connect with other North Americans without having to associate yourself with those pathetic Americans

Adopting the local customs

Wearing native garb just to fit in

Wearing native garb to increase your chances of getting lucky

"When-I-was-in…" stories

Karaoke

Using "expatriate" as a noun

Abbreviating the word expatriate

Getting pierced

Getting a tattoo

That story about how people get robbed on the train by getting knocked out with ether and then wake up—robbed!

Let's Go! (Bonus: reading *Let's Go!* at a train station/by a fountain)

Asking people if they're from the "States"

Asking people if they're from the "UK"

Telling people you're from the "Continent"

Having a continental breakfast

Sleeping bags attached to your pack

Calling all the Germans you meet Nazis

Gambling the last $30 you have in Monte Carlo (Bonus: on roulette)

Spending the last $40 you have in Amsterdam (Bonus: not on a hooker)

Meeting someone on a train

Traveling with that someone

Telling someone they "absolutely must" go somewhere (Bonus: it's Ghana!)

Seeing Big Ben and Parliament for the first time and hitting your pals and saying "Look kids, Big Ben, Parliament building!" (Bonus: thinking it's funny more than once)

Thinking you're going to fall in love (Bonus: just like Julie Delpy and Ethan Hawke in *Before Sunrise!*)

Toe rings

Greasy hair

Two-week goatees

Compasses

Feeling international

Feeling cosmopolitan

Feeling like, thanks to American movies and fast food, it really is just a small world after all

Buying really small toiletry items

Swearing you saw Jesus or an angel in the clouds while flying

Leather necklaces (Bonus: rope bracelets)

The Uffizi (Bonus: the Spanish Steps) (Double Bonus: the Duomo!)

Anything made out of Guatemalan fabric

721. Doing the Can-Can

722. Paper cuts

723. Doodling while talking on the phone

724. Speakerphone!

725. Indicating that you're going to drink something by lifting an imaginary glass toward your mouth

726. Tossin' the cordless

727. Bringing in your pennies to have them counted at the bank

728. When the teller says the pennies come to $8.03, saying, "I'm rich!"

729. Making plates so clean they squeak

730. Making students write an autobiography for their first assignment

731. Extension cords

732. Mini globes

733. Mini-garbage cans

734. Mini refrigerators

735. Fraggle Rock

Bo Derek braids (since you can't blow dry)

Bo Derek braids with beads

Fanny packs (Bonus: really big fanny packs)

Birkenstocks

Tevas

Hiking boots (Bonus: red laces)

Getting drunk on the 4th of July

Spanglish

Franglais

Going to Oktoberfest

Not remembering going to Oktoberfest

Dissing German tourists

Denying that you're an American tourist

Bringing a guitar (Bonus: playing it in the train station!)

Raving on the beach (Bonus: under a full moon!)

Americans living in Prague

Americans living in Prague who start businesses

Americans living in Prague who start magazines

Phallic postcards

All-denim outfits

Australians

Nutella

CAMPING CHEESE

Geo-dome tents

70-below sleeping bags

Sleeping with your girlfriend/boyfriend in your sleeping bag (Bonus: you zip two sleeping bags together) (Double Bonus: saying, "I could get used to this")

Sleeping under the stars

"Packing out" what you "packed in"

Digging a hole and pooping in it, but only 50 feet away from the stream

Mac and cheese

Thinking you'll be able to fish for food

Camping stoves

Campfire songs

Rolling your own smokes

Lighting cigarettes off embers from the fire

Drying your clothes by the fire after you fall in the lake

Spending, like, $500 at the North Face outlet before you go (Bonus: on things you'll never even use, like bungee cords)

Topographic maps (Bonus: knowing how to read them)

Tying your food up in a tree and employing that rock counterbalanced pulley system so the bears can't get at it

S'mores (Bonus: that Gorp shit) (Double Bonus: granola for breakfast, becuase it's, like, *natural*)

Doggie backpacks

Purifying your own water

External frame backpacks

Car-camping (Bonus: Using your headlights to erect your tent when you get there after dark)

Rag wool socks

Mountain climbing shoes

Mushrooms (Bonus: acid!)

Swiss Army knives

Synchilla

Lighter fluid

Flint (Bonus: you brought a Bic, just in case)

ROAD TRIP CHEESE

Chuckling to yourself at other people's speeding tickets

One-arm tans

Running out of gas

Talking to fast-food management guys in the motel sauna

Saying "I can't believe we're really here!"

Making Satanic gestures to children in other cars

Looking for the "real" America

Washing your armpits in a gas station bathroom

Adjusting your accent to accommodate local dialects

Avoiding the rental car mileage charge by disconnecting the odometer

Buying souvenirs

Not buying souvenirs

Being bummed out about driving across Kansas or Nebraska

Taking photographs

Dropping in on an estranged parent

Stealing shit from your motel room

Caverns

Chewing tobacco

Camcorder shots of inanimate objects

Not doing the tourist shit

Doing the tourist shit

Showers that take quarters

Road signs with bullet holes

Taking a picture at each state border

Country music

Making mix tapes before, so you don't have to listen to country

Blending in

Picking up locals

Starting to enjoy the religious stations

Travel logs

Opening a window, smoking a cigarette and having the music really loud (Bonus: you don't even like cigarettes, music or air)

Taking a few minutes to check out the Grand Canyon and then heading on

Judging a state by how clean/dirty their rest area bathrooms are

Rolling down the window, yelping and pretending you're lassoing when you reach a warm climate

Sneaking plants from Nevada into California

Palm Springs streets named after Bob Hope, Dinah Shore and Eisenhower

Old-stars-in-retirement spotting

Getting nervous at state police road blocks

Waving to truck drivers

Fantasizing about never going home

736. Potted plants

737. Mermaids

738. Sandbags

739. Sandbagging someone

740. Growling into the phone

741. Brochures

742. Polar bears wearing sunglasses

743. Cleaning up spills by using your foot to push the towel around

744. Licking your teeth all day after a dentist appointment

745. Stroking your chin when thinking hard

746. Thinking hard

747. All robes

748. All terry cloth

749. Still using those plates you made when you were five

750. Picturing birds dying after getting ensnared by six-pack plastic fasteners that weren't broken apart

sports cheese

You know, America invented sports. It's true. Nobody loves action and adventure and the human drama of the thrill of victory and the agony of defeat like we do. Screw soccer. We love blood, sweat and tears, giving it 110 percent and putting it all out there. Which is not to say we don't always just take it one game at a time, hope the team wins, and thank God and Mom. Sports rock, and we kick ass at 'em. We got our boyz—Michael and Emmit and Shaq and Primetime and The Dream. And they *will* rock you—especially at crunch time. They're who make the pre-game possible. There would be no SportsCenter without our boyz, no tailgating, no Chevy Player of the Game, no Plays of the Week. Sure, there might still be buffalo wings, but there sure as hell wouldn't be any sports bloopers.

Still, we're tough on our boyz. When they suck we put 'em on the DiamondVision and show 30-foot-high instant replays of them sucking. But not only do we hate our boyz when they suck, we hate *ourselves* when they suck. We throw things and scream at the television and say things like, "This ain't fucking tennis!" And we have that right because sports are serious. It's never "only a game." Would we wear matching maroon, gold and teal sweatsuits because of a game? Would we crack high fives till our hands bleed, and name our kids things like Mickey and Willie, or our dogs Isiah, because of a *game*? I think it was FDR who said, "Sports? Fuckin' A!" Without sports life would still be short, but would we play as hard? No sir! There may be no "I" in team, but there is in "Sports—goddamn!"

Mascots

Mascot antics

Mascots frolicking with other mascots

Mascots doing push-ups

Mascots doing push-ups but then giving up after a few, ha ha

Players running into the mascot

Coaches beating up the mascot

Coaches *really* beating up the mascot

The ol' Statue-of-Liberty play

The ol' Lenin's Tomb play

Doing a little dance after a big play

Canadians

Flea-flickers

Golf skirts

Golf shoe tassles

Nose tape

Player-cheerleader relationships

Ski pants

Jokes about the tight end, ha ha

Kickers trying to tackle people

Doing mean things to effigies of the other team

Paying attention during the half-time show

Relish

Strategy

Any team from Ohio

When a football player makes a big play and then tries to get the crowd riled up by flapping his arms up and down

Tailgating

Tailgating without going into the actual game

Cool trademark fan maneuvers (e.g., the "Tomahawk Chop")

Throwin' in the towel

Hangin' up the gloves

"Retiring"

Short sports announcers

Short sports announcers who have never played sports

Short sports announcers who have never played sports getting doused in the locker room after the big win

Asking the player, after the team won the big game, if he thought they'd win

Dog racing

Rooting for a horse/dog without betting any money

Deciding on a horse/dog because its name has personal meaning for you

Jai alai

Sitting in the company seats

751. Holding other people's mail up to the light to see what it says

752. Shaking a present before you open it

753. Saying, "I wonder what this is?" when it's something obvious, like a football, or a spear

754. The ol' baker's dozen

755. Introducing a pet to someone new ("Raymond, Mr. Snuffles, Mr. Snuffles, Raymond.")

756. Chopping wood

757. Getting a truck driver to honk his horn

758. Riding the team bus

759. "Hittin' the hay"

760. "Turning in"

761. "Gettin' some shut-eye"

762. Card tables

763. Accepting Jesus as your personal savior

Castling

Screaming "check!" (Bonus: being wrong)

Pausing to look at your opponent and smirk in between saying "check" and "mate"

Calling the person you're playing against "a pretty tough customer"

Rooks

Yelling out "You sunk my battleship!"

Moving pawns two squares on the first move

Reading chess books

Knowing what Q to R4 means

Chess clubs (Bonus: in elementary school)

Garry Kasparov posters (Bonus: Garry Kasparov dolls)

The Persian Defense

Speed chess

Tables with chessboards painted on them

Puttin' a little pepper on that ball

Pop flies

Soccer teams from places like Surinam

Explaining to someone how soccer is actually called "football" in less developed countries

Out of sheer civic pride, rioting when your team wins the Super Bowl

Punching the goalpost

Punching the goalpost a lot, like you're not only a good football player, but you're some crazy tough boxer guy, too

Believing, just for one second, that professional wrestling is real

"Birdies"

"Bogeys"

Pretending you don't sound like a moron when you're talking about "birdies" and "bogeys"

Sticking your nose in a new can of tennis balls to get the full smell effect

Curling

Chest bumping

Farting on the quarterback's hand when you play center

Flashing the camera the "We're number one" sign even when your team's 1-7

Saying hi to Mom

Saying hi to Dad

Saying hi to your congressional representative

Naming a team after a color

Naming a team something singular, like The Cardinal, whatever the hell that means

Kneepads

Rubbing your friend's head for luck

Deion Sanders (Bonus: *Deion Sanders!*)

Acting injured until the team doctor comes out and then saying "Hey Doc, I'm not hurt, but just stand over me for awhile, and then I'll get up and continue playing like I'm a big hero"

Crying for the camera when you lose

Ordering the *Sports Illustrated* football phone

Parabolic microphones

Knocking dirt off of your shoes with a bat

Applying chalk to your hands for any reason

Handlebar mustaches

Oiling your glove

"Oiling" your "glove"

Spitting on the ball

Foot faults

Adjusting your straps

Missing a tennis shot and adjusting your strings, like the problem was riiiiiight *there*

Walking it off

Playing some bad-ass contact sport and getting driven off the field in a golf cart (Bonus: the golf cart looks like a big football helmet)

Dogs catching frisbees during halftime

Wondering if cheerleaders promote sexism

Being a goalie

Being a goalie with a tricked-out mask

Commercials for football that culminate in exploding helmets

Playing it deep

Electrifying the crowd

Throwing crap onto the field

Throwing some crappy promotional item they gave you when you walked into the stadium onto the field

Blackout under the eyes

Wearing your stirrups high

"Walk is as good as a hit"

"Good eye"

"Take your pitch"

Bringin' it

Buying the program

Buying the program and keeping score

Bedspreads with team logos on them

Redesigning your team's uniforms and casually including black as a team color and subsequently selling lots of hats

Utah

Getting ready to rumble

Getting ready to rhumba

Tales of the tape

The Sweet Science

Sticking and moving

Fighting "out of" any city

Satin robes

Having your name on your shorts

Calling fighters "The Champ"

"Sugar Ray" anyone

Calling fighters "The Kid"

Great White Hopes

764. Accepting Ralph Nader as your personal savior

765. Squirting someone in the crotch to make it look like, you know

766. Inflatable slides that come out of planes

767. Carwash employees who wear uniforms

768. Having different sized/shaped glasses for different drinks

769. Whistles

770. Rock star postage stamps from obscure countries

771. Renting a car

772. Renting a convertible (whee!)

773. Makin' stuff out of pipe cleaners

774. Makin' stuff out of corn cobs

775. Makin' stuff out of clothespins

776. Fine lines

777. Blackmail

123

THE "I'M LOOKING *THIS* WAY, BUT THE BALL'S GONNA GO *THAT* WAY"

THE "THERE'S JUST NO QUESTION ABOUT WHO WE THINK IS THE BETTER TEAM HERE"

THE "THIS REF FORGOT TO TAKE HIS MEDICATION TODAY" REFEREE DISAPPROVAL

THE "MISSED THE SHOT/GOTTA GET THESE STRINGS TIGHTENED"

Batting cleanup (see Corporate Cheese)

Throwin' K's

Throwin' gas

Throwin' games

Throwin' the deuce

Throwin' junk

Doin' junk

Steve Howe

Ivan DeJesus

Buddy Biancalana

Utility infielders

Pitchers with their own personal catchers

Knuckleballers (Bonus: knuckleballers over 50!)

Fielder's choice

Play-by-play guys

Drunk play-by-play guys

Harry Caray

Cameramen who find the hot babe in the crowd

Finding the idiot with face paint/no shirt (Bonus: it's 4 below!)

"Going back to New York" for highlights

Teams that have nicknames for particularly effective portions of the team ("Orange Crush," "Steel Curtain," "The Hogs")

Wearing a mask or costume to the stadium

Student body right

Off-tackles

The hook and ladder

Going to one knee in the end zone

Play action passing

Butt-slapping

Telephones on the sidelines

Talking to your mom on the telephone on the sidelines

Talking to the president on the telephone on the sidelines

Florida State

Calling players "my boyz"

Referring to your team as "we"

John 3:16

Sports where you can't use your hands

Luge

All refs

Refs in shorts

Refs in shorts with weird smiles

Trying to mess up the guy shooting a free throw

Trying to mess up the guy shooting a free throw with a poster of Heather Locklear (pre-"Melrose")

Sneakers with pumps

778. Floral arrangements

779. Natural floral arrangements

780. Dr Pepper

781. Spelling Dr Pepper the correct way, without the period

782. Solar eclipses

783. Knowing when a solar eclipse is going to happen

784. Knowing when a solar eclipse is going to happen in another part of the world

785. Looking at a solar eclipse through one of those boxes with the little hole in it

786. Hitting the pavement

787. Landing on your feet

788. Strokes of genius

789. Rolling credits

790. Star-crossed lovers

791. Picket fences

OVERHEARD AT THE BIG EVENT

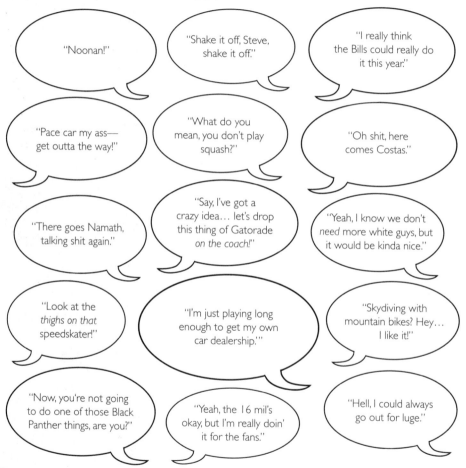

Sneakers with your name on them

Corked bats (Bonus: you pretend like you didn't know!)

Strikers

Sweepers

Cricket bats

Corked cricket bats

Playing touch football, and deciding it would be best if you played a "zone" defense

Picking teams

Being last

Still trying your hardest

Being short, but quick

Do overs

Parquet

Rally caps

Calling ping pong "table tennis"

Calling pool "billiards"

Calling the Knicks a "basketball team"

Having it feel good coming out of your hand

Getting a good look at the basket

Basketball teams from Minnesota

Sports that make use of both guns *and* skis

Dishing

Penetrating

Throwing it off your opponent's leg as you fall out of bounds

Baby sky hooks

Bobsled

Fencing

Screaming "En garde!"

Parrying

Thrusting

Bobby Orr

Hockey coaches storming the ice

Fans that storm the ice

Swedes

Hockey hair

Attempting to break various land speed records, like anyone cares

Trap shooting

Teaching your kids to shoot trap

Waders

Coaching

Jarts

Oversized putters

Peeing in your wetsuit

Peeing in your snowsuit

Being disappointed when your team loses

792. Refrigerators that make noises

793. Top designers

794. Casually referring to the future of retro

795. Giving feedback

796. Staying ahead of the curve

797. Pushing the envelope

798. "Stepping into" the next century

799. Pointing to a piece of fruit or a vegetable and telling a loved one "you're my little cantaloupe!"

800. Love

801. Bums who say "Brother, can you spare a dime?"

802. Celibacy

803. Celibacy "by choice"

804. Chewin 'em up and spitting 'em out

805. Dilating something

806. Cameras that flash twice

WANNABE VERTEBRATE HMMPH!

Captain J. Y. Cousteau

The emperor penguin may be over three feet ta

installment 7
ANIMALS, VEGETABLES, MINERALS, ETC.

cheese on earth

In the beginning, there was God. But before that, there was a thick, primordial ooze that bathed the earth in its smelly, wet, gooey slime. And from this slime came all the organisms we know today: the moss and the lichen, the orangutans and the skinheads, the fishes in the sea and the little birdies in the trees. Exactly how this complex series of events transpired is a matter for the biologists; where God fits in is a matter for Pat Buchanan. Suffice it to say that somewhere in that ooze was contained a double-helix of mitochondrial DNA that would split, and split and split again to beget all the cheese in nature (all cheese in nature is related, just like all residents of West Virginia).

Later—much, much later—there evolved a breed of humans who saw it as their calling in life to explain all this junk, who were compelled—before shuffling off this mortal coil—to give meaning to the wild kingdom, animal behavior and the laws of motion. To let all of us lesser beings understand as they understood. And soon, they were improvising, inventing eyeglasses and naming planets and trying to make cold fusion happen. A few loose cannons among these, perhaps inspired by that lone strand of DNA and all it represented, dreamed up EPCOT and particle accelerators and then… well, you know the rest.

CHEESE NATURALLY OCCURRING IN NATURE

Hummingbirds

Photos of hummingbirds

Hummingbird feeders

Hummingbird feeders designed to look like flowers

The red sugar-water crap you put in hummingbird feeders

Pumice

Muskrats

Otters (Bonus: sea otters!) (Double Bonus: documentaries about sea otters where they repeatedly point out that just like humans, sea otters use tools!)

People who ride goats

Goats that let people ride them

Noises that only dogs can hear

Grists of bees

Drifts of swine

Braces of ducks

Downs of hares

The platypus

Most fish

Flowers sporting thorns or other defense mechanisms (Bonus: the Venus Flytrap!)

Sea cows

Flatworms

Greenland

Radishes

Tsunamis (Bonus: tsunamis caused by volcanoes, underwater earthquakes or mad, evil wizards)

The Kraken

Follicles

Yolk sacs

Lemurs

Ermines

Turtle shit

Being a normal-looking monkey and making fun of the proboscis monkeys because that nose is sooooo stupid

Sea glass

Mollusks

Yorkshire terriers

Plankton

Fruit bats

Huge, bad-ass, four-ton whales that only eat plankton (yeah, right)

Trees that don't change colors in the fall

Arthropoda that aren't insects

Snakes that don't kill anything

Coal (Bonus: the way coal turns into diamonds (suuure it does!))

807. Duds 'n Suds

808. Fluff 'n fold

809. Shake 'n bake

810. Rock 'n bowl

811. Boysenberry

812. Igloos

813. Nougat

814. Macadamia nuts

815. Garbage bags with handles

816. Red pistachios

817. C4 plastique

818. Knowing what C4 plastique is

819. Hot air ballooning (Bonus: hot air balloon *racing!*)

820. Being a (something) enthusiast

821. Being a (something) maven

822. Bloodcurdling screams

823. Smoking cigarettes like James Dean did (Bonus: pretending you didn't know that's how James Dean did it)

Trotting around with a sore mandible all the time

Stirrup iron chafe

Prominent withers

People always checking your teeth

Your father was a sire

Your father was a sire and a *standardbred*

Zebra envy

Knowing that *Equus ferus ferus* is just a single chromosome away

Getting broken by some fat guy

Always being a few hands too short and never quite chestnut enough

Oats for lunch, oats for dinner

Cantering in place at stoplights

Mom was a hinny

The Caspian Sea

Kilimanjaro

Marble

The Nile Delta

Plateaus (Bonus: mesas!)

Weird, cool animals that are extinct, like the Eohippus

Llamas

Strange land masses with mystical names (e.g., "Devil's Tower")

White dwarfs

Maple syrup

Species that are "distant cousins" to another species

Licking your paws

Licking your paws and then wiping your spit on your head to *clean yourself*

Licking someone else's head

Clouds in the shape of teddy bears

Rainbows

Mating calls

Mating dances

Mating, right there, out on the floodplain where everyone can see!

Chablis grapes

Quinoa

Buckwheat

Witch hazel

Thistles

Pine nuts

Hammer toes

Hammerhead sharks

People with webbed feet

Having a waddle or comb

Getting beached

Getting hit by a car

Getting pureed by a jet engine

Getting your foot stuck in a trap set for an animal with much nicer fur than yours

Fertility

Haze that turns pink during the sunset

Swinging from trees

Biped envy

Opposable thumb envy

Dreaming about making fire

Redwood

That hack theory about all the continents having been once connected

Land bridges

Getting all fidgety around the lions

Trying to act all nonchalant when it rains, like you don't even care

Rooting about for something to eat

Evolving so much that you no longer have heavy body hair

Leading the pack

Being the top dog

Being the alpha male

Howling at the moon

Being the early bird (Bonus: getting the worm!)

Being the early bird and still missing out on the worms

Laying eggs

Roosting

Crowing (Bonus: you aren't even a crow)

Making an ant train

Being the guy that breaks from the ant train to look for something besides cereal

Turning around and seeing that everyone is following you to the sugar bowl

Stealing food from a picnic in an ant train

Leeching onto someone

Biting and not letting go

Skunk cheap shots

Losing your sonar and bumping into things

Beef jerky

Growling for no real reason in particular

Stealing food from a picnic in an ant train but the food is too big to fit into your colony (Bonus: it's a ham hock)

Hanging around at the watering hole

Mimicking your parents

Water buffalos

Jacques Cousteau

Birds that all take off at once

Birds that fly into windows and then fall to the ground, ha ha

Licking the backs of toads

Rolling over a log in order to get the big juicy grubs

Carrying your offspring by their necks

Carrying your offspring in your mouth

Carrying your offspring in your pouch

Having a pouch but not really using it

Runts of the litter

Lentils

Those seals that catch air off a jump before they dive into the water

Drinking milk straight from the cow

824. Jets made by Saab

825. Those jets that take off vertically

826. Extreme duress

827. Laser surgery

828. Concept cars (Bonus: *electric* concept cars!)

829. Mail order catalogs that have a little photo of the operator wearing one of those little headset phones (Bonus: she's cute—maybe you'll talk to *her* if you call)

830. Duels

831. Hacking butts

832. Bumming smokes

833. Knowing what a bushing is

834. Bicycle luggage

835. Ordering something from those little ads in the back of a magazine

836. Waxing your chain

837. Baby wipes

838. Gortex

839. Authorized Dealers

Metamorphosing just when you've pretty much got your identity down

Anteaters

Crystals

Carnations

Little boys

Nymphs (heh, heh)

Those "dogs" that peacefully coexist with cats

Flying squirrels

Sea cucumbers

Electric eels

Dogs that carry first-aid supplies around their necks

Dogs that carry casks of liquor around their necks

Dogs that fight crime

Horses that braid their manes

Gorillas that use sign language

Monkeys that wear clothes

Those glow-in-the-dark fish that live in crazy-deep water

Animals that doubled as appliances in prehistoric times

Animals that mate for life

Trees with passageways for cars

Birds that can't fly

Birds that can technically fly, but have a tough time with it

Beavers that communicate to other woodland creatures by paddling a tree with their funny tails

Eating a wild mushroom straight from the ground

Eating a wild mushroom and wondering what kinds of wild mushrooms are the poisonous ones, you know, just for the sake of argument, and then thinking about how you'd find help, being out here in the middle of nowhere all by yourself

Tree frogs

Getting your horns caught in the underbrush

Really little dogs

Fauna

Sea monkeys

Torturing animals more vulnerable than yourself

Being eaten because you are orange and small

Eating your young

Getting domesticated

Wondering where all this trotting around will get you at the end of the day

SCIENCE CHEESE

Alpha Centauri

Communicating with dolphins (Bonus: teaching dolphins the *Close Encounters* song)

Chlorophyll

Mitosis

Phylums

Personal sonar

Zipping out to the Fertile Crescent for a weekend dig

Naming a comet after yourself (Bonus: naming a comet after your sweetie!) (Double Bonus: naming a comet after some fling you met in a bar as a ploy to get in their pants!)

Airplane food

JAMA

NASA

EPCOT

Getting all pissed at the technical inaccuracies in *Apollo 13*

Googols

Memorizing pi past five digits

Hydroponics

Paleontologists

Counting asteroids

Playing Asteroids when you should be counting them

Getting stuck in the air lock of a space ship

Having a favorite gas (Bonus: it's argon!)

Climbing a mountain to check out the weather

Discovering a new species of Protozoa, as if anyone cares

Discovering a new element (Bonus: naming it after your home state)

Looking at the Milky Way and realizing that you *are* pretty insignificant, just like your parents always said

Lysergic acid

Those self-righteous noble gases

Paramecium

Those flags you plant on the moon that look like they're blowing in the wind, but they're not because we are all well aware that there is no air on the moon

Talking about how it's light/dark all the time in Alaska

Believing in the abominable snowman

Tracking the abominable snowman

Calling him the Yeti

Owning a weather balloon

840. Amusement park rides designed to get you wet

841. Taking the money and running

842. Having grace under fire

843. Having grace in a fire

844. Foreign language tapes

845. Linoleum designed to look like bricks

846. Participles

847. Pronouns

848. Big toenails

849. Rhyming your quatrains

850. Crime scenes

851. "How to get published" books

852. Writing what you know

853. Listening to your heart

854. Realizing your dreams

855. Actualizing your dreams

being a god cheese

Slumming with the humans

Turning into a swan and making it with some babe

Turning into a shower of gold and making it with some babe in a tower

Flooding the earth for forty days and forty nights

Hurling thunderbolts

Smiting heathens

Exalting the humble and meek

Destroying cities like so many sand castles

Walking on water

Getting goats sacrificed to you

Getting virgins sacrificed to you

Telling some guy to sacrifice his son to you on a dare (Bonus: forgetting to tell him you're not serious)

Creating the duck-billed platypus, just to see what it would look like

Listening to all the debates about whether the tomato is a fruit or a vegetable, as if you care

Rising from your own ashes

Taking off your belt to learn Jesus some manners

Chewing your sacred cud

Having your own day

Taking your name in vain

Making creatures in your own image

Turning regular folk into pillars of salt

Flowing robes

Overuse of plagues

Not really giving a damn when people fast in your honor

Making some guy spend his whole life in a cave on the Arabian peninsula writing down exactly what you say, like you weren't just making it up as you went along

Starting a new religion every thousand years—just to stay fresh

Angels waiting on you, hand and foot

Omniscience

Ambrosia *again?*

Say, that was a pretty good hymn.

I know that. I know everything, you dolt!

136

Owning a mountaintop observatory

Owning an atom smasher

Walking around all the time in one of those poly-blend lab coats

Wearing it to bed

The Periodic Table (Bonus: chanting the Periodic Table while doing laundry or taking a shower)

That new airport in Denver

The Andromeda Galaxy (Bonus: *The Andromeda Strain*)

Whale studies

Mitochondria

Spending your evenings in the lab trying to clone yourself a kid

Charcoal tablets

Benzene rings

Absolute values

Latin directions on pharmaceuticals (e.g., bis die, ante cibum, ad libitum)

Accelerating particles

Counting electrons

Exposing people to viruses to protect them

Zygotes

Blastocysts

"In Search Of"

Documentaries where the producers put a tarantula and a scorpion in an aquarium and pretend it's the desert

Narrators whispering crap about the cycle of life while they're killing each other

Genetically engineered tomatoes

Claiming genetically engineered tomatoes taste better

Fast-breeder nuclear reactors

Plate tectonics

Owning a thermometer that measures Kelvins

Having to keep the eyewash near at all times

Thinking that the troposphere is a generally underrated layer of the atmosphere

Quarks

Nutrinos

The Greenhouse Effect

Calling bullshit on the so-called Greenhouse Effect

Yelling "Eureka" when you discover something, even though it's just some lame town in California

856. Dreaming of food

857. Dreaming of sex

858. Writers' workshops

859. Staying in character

860. "Realism"

861. Mind control

862. Alien mind control

863. Jedi mind control

864. Uncut videos

865. Radar detectors

866. Classic lines

867. Slimming down

868. Trimming down

869. Paralegals

870. Living life to the fullest

871. The curtains in hearses

872. Calling it curtains

873. Tearful farewells

874. Crying at the end

875. Plodding through some crappy, seemingly endless book that doesn't even have an ending and still crying at the end

WRITTEN AND EDITED BY
Dave Eggers
Dave Moodie
Lance Crapo
Marny Requa
Zev Borow
Paul Tullis
Nancy Miller

STAFF
Rebecca Gold, Betsy Pollert, Lisa Salmon, Ursula Guise,
Jason Adams, Erika Buck

OTHER CONTRIBUTORS
Barb Bersche, Dave Boyer, Tina Caputo, Nicole Harb, Dave Hayes, Brent Hoff,
Gabe Levy, Martha McPartlin, David Mills, Matt Ness, Neal Pollack, Ted Rall,
Blake Robin, Larry Smith, Flagg Taylor

ART
Marcos Sorensen (chapter illustrations), Bart Nagel (cover cheese photo),
Dan Perkins (back-to-back conversing couple cartoon)

STARRING
Karen Covington (as the girl mime)
Christopher Pelham-Fence (as the boy mime)
& Sister Mary Ignatius (as "The Nun")